ISRAEL AND THE PALESTINIANS

ISRAEL AND THE PALESTINIANS

COUNTRIES IN CRISIS

Edited by

MARTIN WRIGHT

**Contributors: Paul Cossali, Roger Hardy,
Lawrence Joffe, Noah Lucas, David McDowall,
Elfi Pallis, Martin Wright**

St J

ST. JAMES PRESS
CHICAGO AND LONDON

ISRAEL AND THE PALESTINIANS

Published by Longman Group UK Limited,
Westgate House, The High, Harlow, Essex CM20 1YR, UK.
Telephone (0279) 442601
Telex 81491 Padlog
Facsimile (0279) 444501

Published in the United States and Canada by St James Press,
233 East Ontario St, Chicago 60611, Illinois, U.S.A.

ISBN 0-582-05156-8 (Longman, hard cover)
       0-582-05160-6 (Longman, paper cover)
           1-558-62030-3 (St James)

First published in 1989

22704740

British Library Cataloguing in Publication Data
Wright, Martin *1958-*
Israel and the Palestinians.—(Countries in crisis).
1. Israel. Conflict, 1945—with Palestinian Arabs
I. Title II. Series
956'.04

ISBN 0–582–05156–8
ISBN 0–582–05160–6 pbk

Phototypeset by Quorn Selective Repro Ltd, Loughborough, Leics.
Printed and bound in Great Britain by
Biddles Ltd, Guildford and King's Lynn

CONTENTS

ABOUT THE AUTHORS

Paul Cossali is co-author of *Stateless in Gaza* (Zed Books, 1986). He has lived and worked in the Gaza Strip and elsewhere in the Middle East.

Roger Hardy was formerly Editor of *Middle East* magazine, and is currently working as Middle Eastern Specialist at the BBC World Service.

Lawrence Joffe is a freelance writer who has travelled widely in Israel. He contributed to the *Chronicle of the 20th Century* (Longman, 1988).

Noah Lucas is Fellow in Israeli Studies at the Oxford Hebrew Centre. Formerly on the staff of the University of Sheffield and the Hebrew University in Jerusalem, he is the author of *The Modern History of Israel* (Weidenfeld and Nicholson, 1975).

David McDowall is a freelance writer who has specialized in Palestinian issues. He is author of *Palestine and Israel: The Uprising and Beyond.* (I.B. Tauris, June 1989) and of the Minority Rights Group report *The Palestinians*.

Elfi Pallis is an Israeli journalist living in London. She has written on Israeli affairs for various newspapers and magazines, and edits the *Israeli Mirror*.

Martin Wright is editor of the *Countries in Crisis* series. Formerly a writer on Middle Eastern affairs for *Keesing's Record of World Events*, he now works as a publishing consultant and freelance journalist.

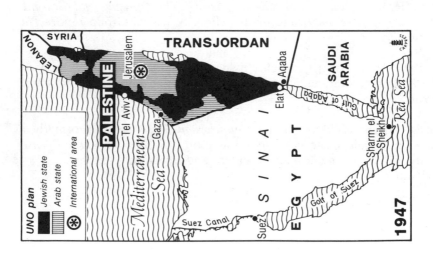

Israel and the Occupied Territories

The UN Partition Plan, 1947

PREFACE

The Palestinian uprising, which exploded out of Gaza and onto the world's television screens at the end of 1987, has thrown the Arab-Israeli conflict back into the headlines and onto the international political agenda.

Israel or Palestine—or, as some hope, both, the biblical Promised Land has for many been a land of broken promises and of hopes betrayed. This book delves back 2,000 years into the origins of this oldest of conflicts, and provides a clear, detailed account of its twists and turns, from the first stirrings of Zionism last century, through the growing tension of the 1920s and '30s under the British mandate; the birth of Israel and its battle to survive in four fierce, brief wars; the growth of Arab terrorism and Palestinian resistance; the "false dawn" of Camp David; the invasion of Lebanon and the splits within the PLO; to the close of the '80s, with Israel divided over how to respond both to the olive branch of recognition offered by the PLO, and to the volley of stones flung by the children of the camps.

In Part II, leading commentators examine the critical choices facing Israelis and Palestinians alike, and assess the prospects for any lasting settlement, while Reportage features go behind the headlines to give a glimpse of the impact of events on everyday life.

Acknowledgements. The Editor wishes to extend his thanks to Roger East and Neil Hicks for their advice and support in the initial stages of the project.

The front cover photos, by John Chapman (Israeli troops) and David Harden (Palestinian youths) were provided by the Select Photo Agency. The text photos are by John Tordai and Martin Wright. The maps on page viii were supplied by Carpress International Press Agency. In all cases, copyright rests with the photographers/agencies.

ISRAEL: INFRASTRUCTURE

Today Israel is a contested land. Situated at the nexus of Africa and Asia, Israel is tiny—20,000 square kilometres, or half the size of Wales—and lacks natural resources. Yet every neighbouring Arab state, apart from Egypt since 1979, is in theory at least committed to her destruction.

The present-day state is bordered by Lebanon and Syria to its north, Jordan to its east, and the Sinai desert (now part of Egypt) to the south. Since 1967 Israel has also occupied the Golan Heights, the Gaza Strip and the West Bank of the River Jordan (claimed by some Jews as the biblical Land of Israel, (*Eretz Yisrael*). These territories make up 7,460 square kilometres.

It has an extremely varied geography and climate. The altitude ranges from 1,300 m at Mt Azmon to 422 m below sea-level at the Dead Sea. Apart from a small strip on the Gulf of Aqaba, most of the coastline lies on the Mediterranean Sea. The northern coastal plain opens out onto the Plain of Sharon; to the south are the valleys of Jezreel and Hulveh, a reclaimed swampland. Inland the hilly Galilee region dips down to Lake Tiberias and eastwards to the hills of Samaria and Judaea on the West Bank. The Negev desert to the south makes up 60 per cent of the total land area. Much of its northern sector has recently been cultivated. Coastal dwellers enjoy a hot but temperate climate, with more rain to the north. Inland temperatures are markedly cooler, with occasional snow.

Tel Aviv, founded in 1909, is the biggest city and centre of industry; Haifa in the north vies with Tel Aviv–Jaffa as the main port. Jerusalem has been declared the capital but has not been recognized as such by the international community, which maintains its diplomatic presence in Tel Aviv. Israel won the eastern sector of the city from Jordan in the 1967 war, and annexed both it and the Golan Heights (bordering Syria in the north-east). Major towns in the West Bank include Nablus, Hebron, Bethlehem, Ramallah and the world's oldest surviving walled city, Jericho.

Agriculture and industry employ millions of Israelis through the *Histradut*, a trade union/state corporation. A minority work on kibbutzim, communal farming settlements, which produce a disproportionately large percentage of Israel's crops. Today Israel is a leading fruit exporter, especially of citrus and avocado pears, and is self-sufficient in dairy produce, vegetables and fodder. Industry is advanced for the region; much is based around military production. Service industries account for more than half the employment in Israel, and tourism is another source of income. Palestinians in the occupied territories work as farmers, in light industry and in the service sector. Many commute daily to jobs in Israel. The Palestinian economy in the territories is restricted by a range of Israeli regulations.

Politically, Israel is a multi-party democracy with proportional representation elections. Palestinians in the occupied territories have no political representation. Most education in Israel is provided by some 3,320 state schools (divided into Hebrew secular, Hebrew religious and Arab secular). With 64,000 university students, Israel has proportionately the third highest college enrolment in the world. A high percentage of Palestinians attend universities in the West Bank and Gaza.

Israelis make up a fifth of the world's Jewish population. Although Israel was founded on immigration with one and a half million arriving between independence and the mid-1970s, today most of her citizens were born in the land. The people of Israel are extremely diverse. Jews reflect the racial origins of the regions they came from; East European Jews are often fairer, with blue eyes; Moroccans are olive-complexioned and curly-haired; Yemenites are tall, dark and slender; Ethiopian Jews are black. Today more than half of Israel's Jewish population is oriental or Sephardic in origin.

Similarly, Palestinian Arabs show different origins: the southern bedouins appear darker and have pronounced Semitic features; in the north Palestinians and Druze have fairer complexions, showing traces of Philistine, Crusader and even ancient Israelite blood.

More Jews and Palestinians live outside their "common land" than in it. Jews form the majority in the state proper, but if the occupied territories are included (with their population of 1.5 million), it is predicted that Arabs will form the majority by the first decade of the next century. In the context of the Middle East, Israelis emphasize their minority status (3.5 million Jews versus some 120 million Arabs); within Israel, Arabs stress theirs. As for the exiled Palestinians, they long for a return to Palestine with all the fervour of the early Zionists.

An Israeli West Bank settlement at Ma'ale Adumim (*Martin Wright*)

REPORTAGE

SUNSHINE AND STONES IN SHATI CAMP

Paul Cossali

On the edge of Shati ("Beach") camp, a knot of small boys is crouching behind a low wall. They are talking in hushed, urgent tones, too absorbed even to be distracted by the presence of foreign journalists. One of them is holding a palm sized fragment of mirror which he tilts to the late afternoon sun. He directs the ray towards a tall building that stands 100 metres away, high above the squat labyrinth of refugee shelters. Once there it joins half a dozen other pinpricks of light, and together they dance up the side of the building to the uniformed figures standing on the rooftop. For half a minute, as the lights dart around the figures, the little shaven heads cluster together. Not a word is spoken. Suddenly there is a sharp crack of automatic gunfire. The boys duck behind the wall, let out whoops of delight and do an impromptu victory jig in the sand. Almost immediately a high pitched whistling erupts from other parts of the camp. A runny nosed 8-year-old steps from behind the wall, shouts something unintelligible and lets a stone fly from a crude slingshot.

As the mirror changes hands for the game to start again a teenager approaches and invites us to accompany him. He leads us towards the centre of the camp, down sandy tracks cut by open sewers and past piles of rotting garbage patrolled by clouds of angry flies. Tattered Palestinian flags hang from overhead powerlines and every wall serves as an *intifada* billboard. There's very little in the way of revolutionary sloganeering. Most of the graffiti detail forthcoming strikes, dates of "escalating confrontation" and urgings to participate in the popular committees. "Abu Mahmoud," reads one, "Cease your criminal activities. We are watching you." It's signed by the Palestinian Popular Army.

We take a left turn through a narrow alley which twists and turns towards the southern edge of the camp. Eventually we come to a clearing in the maze. Twenty or so youths, the youngest 12 and the eldest 15 or 16, are ranged on either side of the street hurling rocks at an unseen target. On the far side a man in his 30s is clambering over the ruins of a demolished shelter. He shouts instructions to his younger comrades and hands down breezeblocks which are quickly collected and smashed on the roadside. None of the youths is masked and a couple run towards us shouting, "No pictures, no pictures!" A lanky teenager takes me by the arm, pokes his head up the street and motions me towards the older man on the other side. He in turn introduces himself as Ahmed and ushers us a short way down an alley where he politely requests identification. Passports and press cards are scrutinized and returned.

Ahmed explains that a couple of army jeeps are stationed a short way up the street. The youths want to entice them into the clearing, but Ahmed doesn't think they'll be drawn. There's no space for their jeeps to turn round and he's sure they're too frightened to come on foot. I say people have described Shati as "liberated territory". He smiles broadly. "Maybe half liberated. The army hasn't patrolled the centre and north of the camp during the day for more than a month, but there are always confrontations in this part. And at night they come to make arrests, but they have to come in big convoys. It's the same when they want to impose a curfew."

Our conversation is interrupted by a loud bang which sends a volley of steel marbles ricocheting down the street. For a moment the stone throwers take shelter behind the walls, only to re-emerge with a barrage of jeers and rocks. Seconds later a warning is shouted. Ahmed pulls me to the ground and motions for me to cover my ears. The world shakes with a deafening explosion. "Percussion grenade," says Ahmed, still smiling. He taps the nearest boy on the shoulder and the youth darts into the road, ducking and weaving to collect the spent grenade and as many steel marbles as he can find. Back in the safety of the alleys they're handed around like sweets.

Ahmed announces it's time for him to leave. "I have business elsewhere. The youths will talk to you." He shouts a farewell and jogs into the maze. Some of the elder boys shuffle into a semi-circle, ordering the younger ones to keep up the stone throwing. Many of them are wearing T-shirts with political motifs; an index finger pointing skyward above Jerusalem's Dome of the Rock mosque, a favourite symbol of the Islamic Resistance Movement *Hamas*, or else the more obviously nationalist "Palestine" written in English above a stylized olive tree with "I love you Palestine" in Arabic underneath. One has a faded Guevara across his skinny chest.

It prompts a question about their political allegiances. Are they supporters of the pro-PLO United Leadership or one of the Islamic organizations? It's not a popular question. "We're all one," exclaims the lanky youth to a chorus of agreement, "We are all Palestinians and we're all Moslems. It doesn't matter if he's *Hamas*, he's Jihad and I'm PLO. We are all against the occupation, against the Shamir autonomy plan. We are all prepared to be martyrs for the *intifada* and for a Palestinian state. We will fight to liberate our land with these," he profers clenched hands full of broken breeze block. His eyes are ablaze with passion and his words trip over each other in a fierce torrent, but when he's finished his comrades give him a spontaneous burst of applause. They begin chanting "In blood, in spirit, we will redeem you O Palestine!" and throw their stones with renewed vigour.

PART I: HISTORICAL SURVEY

WHOSE LAND?

ORIGIN OF THE JEWS (2,500 BC–69 AD)

Judaism is essentially the religion of ethical monotheism—the belief that one God made the world, and created man to help complete his plan. This belief is central to Christianity and Islam too, but Judaism differs in ascribing to the Jewish people a special role in the unfolding history of the world, to be "a light unto the nations" but also "a peculiar people". Herein is a source of the jealousy of a non-Jewish world, whose anti-Semitism proved the final prompting of a Jewish yearning to return to the Land. Modern Zionism—the restoration of Jewish statehood—was seen as a cure to this malady.

According to the Bible, Abraham founded Judaism and the Jewish people at God's behest almost 2,000 years before Christ. (The stories in the 24 books of the Jewish Torah, regarded by Christians as their Old Testament, bear some similarity to those in the Moslem Koran). The land promised to them was then called Canaan. Like the Arabs, the ancient Jews were probably a Semitic people made up of nomadic tribes and speaking a language called Hebrew, still used in Israel today.

Returning from exile in Egypt under Moses, the Jews founded the Judaean state composed of the 12 Tribes. First they had to subdue the older inhabitants, Baal-worshipping Canaanites, and newer invaders from the sea, the Semitic Philistines (later the Romans adapted the word Philistine to call the province "Palestrina", from which came the present name Palestine). In time Jerusalem became the capital of Judaea. Saul, David and Solomon set up a monarchy, but ultimately God's laws ruled via a *Nasi* (judge).

Then, as now, Israel (a collective name for the 12 tribes, and another name of the patriarch Jacob) was a small force, buffeted by the superpowers of the day—Egypt, Assyria, the Hittites, Greece and finally Rome. Assyrians wiped out 10 of the tribes in 721 BC; Babylonians took the rest into exile in 586 BC. The earliest liturgy of a desire to return to "The Promised Land" was written then.

The Jews were permitted to return by Cyrus II of Persia and to rebuild their Temple, only to be conquered by Greeks in 333 BC. In 63 BC Romans ruled the Kingdom of Judaea as part of "Palestrina", but allowed Jewish autonomy under various puppet kings. One estimate suggests that there were at that time as many as three million Jews inside the land and five million outside.

JERUSALEM IS FALLEN (AD 70–569)

Soon tensions arose within an increasingly rigorous *Sanhedrin* (religious authority); and between them and the increasingly assimilated Hellenistic kings. Messianic sects flourished, of which the followers of Jesus of Nazareth were one. (In time they formed a distinct religion, Christianity). The first Jewish revolt broke out in 66 AD; Jerusalem was sacked by the Romans four years later. The last outpost, Masada (still a potent Jewish nationalist symbol) fell in 73 AD. A second rebellion was crushed in 138 AD, at the cost of nearly 600,000 Jewish lives (according to the contemporary Roman historian Tacitus). In all, Jews had ruled themselves on and off for 1,300 years.

Having lost their statehood, the Jews turned inward, forming a community government under the *Sanhedrin*. Rabbis began codifying the Oral Law into the Talmud, which formed the constitution of Jewish life wherever Jews travelled. Dispersed Palestinian Jews found refuge among their Diaspora brethren in the Roman Empire and beyond, in Persia and India.

When Rome adopted Christianity as the state religion in the fourth century, life grew harder for Jews. The converted pagans now accused them of responsibility for the death of Christ. Nonetheless, the Jews had become indispensable as traders.

At the same time continuous barbarian invasions sapped the strength of the Roman empire. Rome was repeatedly sacked, and the last western emperor Augustus Justinian was ousted in 568 AD. The eastern empire, however, continued under Byzantine Christian rule and included Palestine. As Europe entered the so-called Dark Ages the religion of Islam emerged to revitalize the Middle East.

THE BIRTH OF ISLAM AND CONQUEST OF PALESTINE, 570–1291

The founder of Islam was the prophet Mohammed. Born in 570 AD in Mecca, in the Hejaz region of Arabia, he moulded a faith which absorbed elements of Christianity and Judaism, but wrote a new holy book, the Koran. Originally adopted by the surrounding nomadic Arab tribes, Islam soon spread far beyond its epicentre so that today one seventh of all people are Moslems. In Islam, all history pre-Mohammed is called *Jahiliya*, the period of ignorance; armed with this concept, Moslem politicians often paper over national differences with a notion of the unity of the Moslem, and by extension Arab, people. Another concept, Jihad or Holy War, serves to justify the reconquest of any land which was ever Moslem.

In 636 AD—just two years after the prophet's death—Jerusalem fell to the Arabs. Some 300,000 Jews lived in Palestine at the time, now called "Falastin" on the West Bank of the Jordan and "Urdun" on the East. Many Jews converted to Islam and adopted the Arabic language, though others stayed true to their original faith. After Mecca and Medina, Jerusalem became the third holiest site to Moslems; they built the Mosque of al-Aqsa and Dome of the Rock where the Jewish Temple had stood, from which site it is said Mohammed rose to heaven.

Within 100 years the Islamic empire stretched from Spain in the west to China in the east. But divisions between contending caliphate dynasties (exacerbated by Shia and Sunni religious splits) opened the door to the resurgent Christian Crusaders of Europe who sacked Jerusalem in 1099, massacring Jews and Moslems alike. In 1187 the Moslem Abbayid leader Salah al-Din recaptured the city and destroyed the Christian principality of Palestine.

Later Crusaders regained the land for a while, but in 1291 Egyptian Mamelukes took Palestine for Islam, defeating the last Christian rulers of the Holy Land. In the fourteenth century, a new Moslem resurgence began, but without the Arabs; soon Ottoman Turks following orthodox Sunni Islam faced a hostile Persian Shia Safavid empire, and North Indian Mughals. The Ottomans took Jerusalem in 1517. It became part of Falastin, a region (*vilayet*) within the Ottoman province of Syria with Ramlah as its capital. It remained so until the Ottoman collapse in 1918.

Equality before Allah (God) is a central tenet of faith for all Moslem believers, but Islam often discriminated against "pagans". Jews and Christians, however, had special status as People of the Book (*Um ha-Kitab*). As such they paid *dhimmi*, a special tax, to mark them off from "true believers", but at a sultan's discretion they could reach great heights. Compared to Christian Europe at the time, Palestine's Moslem rulers were more tolerant to Jews. This encouraged some Jewish immigration to the land. By the sixteenth century an estimated 10,000 Jews lived in the area of Safed, though they remained a small minority.

DIASPORA JEWRY, 1290–1896

Jews thrived under Moslem rule in Spain, but their co-religionists in Christian Europe suffered under numerous papal edicts. In England large numbers of Jews were expelled in 1290 after persecutions of varying ferocity. Although active as financiers, their status was at best precarious, and many died in vicious pogroms. In time, Jews divided into different groups. Those under Moslem rule were Sephardim; others who lived in central and western Europe were Ashkenazi. Separate communities lived in Yemen, Ethiopia, India and even China.

By the twelfth century most European Jews had moved into northern Russia, and spoke Yiddish based on Old German, but with Hebrew infusions. These Jews were forced to live in special quarters called ghettos; many Jews in Moslem countries were similarly restricted to *mellahs*. With the final defeat of the Spanish Moslems by Christians in 1492, all Jews who would not convert to Christianity were expelled.

The centres of Jewish learning spread to Europe; but their vulnerability to attacks prompted feelings of insecurity, which in turn were exploited by a number of "false messiahs". Most prominent of these was Shabbtai Tzvi, who like several others inserted a Zionist theme, promising a return to the Holy Land.

In northern Russia and the Baltic states, meanwhile, a restrictive Pale of Settlement was set up for Jews. Following the European Age of Enlightenment in the eighteenth and nineteenth centuries, however, Jews felt safer. Many escaped the strictures of the ghetto and the Pale to join Gentile society. Yet ironically some Jews saw this "liberation" as a danger. To Ahad ha-Am, an early Zionist writer, such "assimilation" threatened Jewish survival, and he called for a return to Palestine to rebuild a Jewish spiritual centre.

In Europe's more feudal areas Jews still found themselves victims of pogroms and massacres. After a particularly vicious spate in 1881 Jewish groups called Bilu emigrated from Russia to Palestine, in what is known as the First Aliyah (literally, ascent). For most Russian Jews, however, the USA was the new Promised Land. From 1880 to 1914 two million emigrated there, while only 60,000 went to Palestine.

The apparent security of German and French Jews was disturbed in 1894 by the Dreyfus Case, when a Jewish French army officer, Alfred Dreyfus, was wrongly accused of treason. Shocked by this ugly face of anti-Semitism, Theodore Herzl, an Austrian journalist and assimilated Jew, initiated the Zionist revival. The first Zionist Congress met in Basle, Switzerland, in 1897.

Unlike previous Zionists, Herzl's appeal (as described in his 1896 book *Judenstaat*) was based on a secular nationalism such as Garibaldi's in Italy, not on biblical Messianism. In his view a Jewish state would "normalize" the Jewish condition, and give them the security they lacked under foreign rulers.

Palestine was Herzl's first choice for a homeland because of its historical associations with the Jewish people, and because there had been a continuous Jewish presence there, albeit small, since the Roman destruction. He played down the Arab presence there, seeing them as a largely nomadic people with shallow roots in Palestine *per se*, and affiliations to the larger Arab world. Present-day Arab historians dispute this view, pointing to a "unique Palestinian identity" fostered by a growing urban minority. They concede there was no Palestinian state, but say this was true of Turkish provinces throughout the region. Palestinians, they say, exercised limited autonomy under the Turks via parastatal bodies like the Supreme Moslem Council.

JEWISH RETURN, ARAB RESISTANCE, 1897–1917

Britain had colonial aspirations in the Middle East at this time, with an eye on the oilfields of Persia and security of passage through the Suez Canal in Egypt; so Herzl approached London about the possibility of Jewish settlement in Palestine. Instead in 1903 Britain suggested an area of Uganda as a Jewish homeland. The expedient Herzl seemed prepared to accept this offer, but in 1905 Zionist delegates rejected it. Negotiations for settlement in Palestine began with the Turkish Sultan, but in vain.

Meanwhile the Jewish population of Palestine grew from 25,000 in 1880 to 90,000 in 1914. Despite Arab numerical preponderance (estimated at between 150,000 and 450,000 in 1880) the bedrock of a Jewish state was formed. In 1864 archaeologists began excavating ancient Jewish sites; in 1881, Eliezer Ben Yehuda revived the Hebrew language; in 1909 Tel Aviv, the first all-Jewish city, was built. The Second Aliyah (1904–1914) brought 40,000 new Jews, and saw the foundation of today's Israeli political parties. Jews began the piecemeal purchase of land mainly from absentee Arab landlords living in Lebanon.

The reaction of Palestine's Arabs to the newcomers was mixed. Some welcomed the economic revival they brought; others were suspicious—in 1891 some Arab notables in Jerusalem asked the Ottomans to ban Jewish land purchase and immigration; Arab newspaper articles warned their leaders to imitate Zionist organization or lose out to them; 11 Jewish settlements were attacked in the period till 1914, in which year anti-Zionist groups were founded in Jaffa, Haifa and Jerusalem. In 1905 a far-sighted Lebanese Arab, Najib Azuri, wrote in a French Arabic paper: "The reawakening of the Arab nation and the growing Jewish efforts at rebuilding the ancient monarchy of Israel on a very large scale—these two movements are destined to fight each other continually, until one of them triumphs . . .".

Arab intellectuals in the *al-Fatat* (Young Girl) organization, spread throughout the Turkish-ruled Middle East, plotted to rid their lands of their overlords. Many were inspired by the same nationalistic and socialistic sentiments as the early Zionists. They rejected what they saw as the feudal backwardness of Ottoman rule, and dreamt of a new pan-Arab identity bolstered by Western-style "modernization". By the end of the nineteenth century, however, Western states had colonized Arab lands west of Suez; here, and especially in Egypt, an anti-Western Muslim revival inspired local nationalists. The religious–secular schism still pervades Arab political philosophies today. Later, as colonialist powers left the Middle East, Zionism and Israel became the focus of Arab nationalists' opposition.

When World War One broke out, Arab and Jewish legions joined the British army to help fight the Turks, who had allied with Austro-German forces. The Emir Feisal ibn Hussein wanted to lead a united Arab Nation, and Britain sent Colonel T.E. Lawrence to help him drive the Turks out of Syria and Iraq.

DISMEMBERING THE TURKISH TERRITORIES, 1918–1920

British forces took Jerusalem in December 1917. By 1918 the war was over and the Turks were routed (the Ottoman caliphate formally ended in 1924). Now was the time to unravel the conflicting promises made during these four years of war.

What resulted was a period of intense bargaining between the British and the French, both victorious powers in the war who had regional strategic interests in the Middle East. In secret letters written by Sir Henry McMahon, British High Commissioner in Cairo, during 1915 and 1916, Hussein, Hashemite Sharif of Mecca and father to Feisal, was promised a vast Arab state if he helped defeat the Turks. There was, however, no clear agreement over precise borders, and no specific mention was made of Palestine.

Meanwhile in 1916 British and French diplomats, Sir Mark Sykes and Georges Picot respectively, signed a secret agreement which undermined the McMahon letters by seeking to divide the area into spheres of influence for each country. It planned to hand Syria to France, Transjordan to Britain and "the Holy Land" of Palestine to be shared between France, Britain and Russia. General Allenby, who had led the British conquest of 1917, seemed to promise Palestine's Arabs some measure of self-rule in 1919, adding to the confusion. Some Palestinian leaders thought their destiny lay with the Hashemite claims to a Greater Syria which traditionally encompassed the province of Palestine.

For the Zionists, however, intensive lobbying of the British foreign secretary, Lord Arthur Balfour, by their chairman, Chaim Weizman, a Russian-born British chemist, had led to the British Balfour Declaration of Nov. 2, 1917. It stated: "His Majesty's government views with favour the establishment in Palestine of a national home for the Jewish people, and will use their best endeavours to facilitate the achievement of this object, it being clearly understood that nothing shall be done which may prejudice the civil and religious rights of non-Jewish communities in Palestine or the rights and political status of Jews in any other country".

Zionists welcomed this recognition, albeit limited; but Britain saw matters in a regional context. In 1918 Britain recognized Hussein as King of the Arabian Hejaz. In 1919 his son Feisal (later King of Iraq) met Weizman and signed a co-operation agreement. Later he wrote to American Zionist Felix Frankfurter: "We [educated Arabs] wish the Jews a hearty welcome home . . . we are working together for a reformed and revised Near East, and our two movements complement one another . . . . There is room in Syria for us both. Indeed, I think that neither can be a success without the other."

His optimism was not universally shared. In the USA the Presidential King–Crane Commission warned that "Zionists looked forward to a practically complete dispossession of the present non-Jewish inhabitants of Palestine . . . a gross violation of the principle of [self-determination]".

BRITISH MANDATE—SITTING ON A POWDERKEG, 1921–1929

In April 1920 the victors of World War One called a conference at San Remo in Italy to agree on new boundaries in the Middle East. It awarded Britain mandates over Palestine and Iraq, ratified by the League of Nations in 1922. By so doing the League seemed to contradict the principle on which it was founded, namely the right to self-determination of all peoples. Over the ensuing years radical Arabs began agitating against the Western presence in the region. In Palestine, many saw the Jews as clients of the West. For their part most Zionists considered themselves as neither East nor West, but as pioneers redressing their dispossession from their land 2,000 years earlier.

Sir Herbert Samuel, a British Jew, was appointed High Commissioner of Palestine. In 1921 Transjordan was hived off from the rest of Palestine (though remained part of the British mandate) and awarded to Feisal's brother, Abdullah, by Franco-British agreement. Britain and France agreed that no Jews could settle east of the Jordan River. In 1922 France declared a mandate over Syria, to the chagrin of Feisal who considered it his. In short, Britain and France between them now controlled all of what is today Lebanon, Israel, Jordan, Syria and Iraq, leaving south Arabia as a nominally independent Arab territory.

The Palestine mandate's declared aim was to "put into effect" the 1917 Balfour Declaration, but unlike the other mandates it provided no specific agenda for achieving independence. It did, however, guarantee the establishment of a Jewish national home (the first time an international document had done so); aim to safeguard the civil and religious rights of all inhabitants; and support Jewish immigration "under suitable conditions". It offered by law citizenship to all Jews who settled permanently in Palestine, and called for a Jewish Agency to advise Britain on Jewish settlement on "state lands and waste lands".

Zionist settlers meanwhile continued using the funds of Diaspora benefactors, channelled through the Jewish National Fund, to buy land in Palestine from Arab landlords. Feeling threatened by this, other Arabs turned to violence. In 1920 Haj Amin al-Husseini, newly appointed as head of the Supreme Moslem Council, claimed the Jews were trying to take over the Holy Places in Jerusalem. A riot ensued there during the Moslem festival of Nabi Musa, killing six Jews and six Arabs. Elsewhere Arabs attacked Jewish settlements, and after a raid in June near the Sea of Galilee the Jews set up a defence force, the *Hagana*, under the auspices of the newly formed *Histadrut* trade union. Though small-scale, it marked a change from the watchmen who since 1908 had guarded against sporadic small-scale raids by rural assailants.

In 1921 Haj Amin's control over Palestinian politics was bolstered by his appointment as *mufti* of Jerusalem, effectively the spiritual leader of the Moslems in Palestine. That same year renewed Arab unrest in Jaffa cost the lives of 47 Jews. Arabs demanded a limit on Jewish immigration and land purchase. Their sense of betrayal by Britain is well illustrated in the poetry of the time. The growing conflict in Palestine exacerbated tensions between Jews and Arabs elsewhere in the Middle East.

But Palestinian Arabs lacked an organized popular political leadership. While the majority *fellahin* (peasants) lived in villages, traditional leadership lay with old Jerusalem families of notables, like the Nashashibis, Nusseibehs, Khalidis and Husseinis. Wrought by age-old rivalries, they were also tainted by collaboration with foreign rulers, most recently Turks.

By contrast Zionist groups enjoyed mass affiliations among Jewish settlers. They divided into socialist and nationalist camps (the religious Mizrachi Zionists were a distinct minority) but co-operated on the twin aims of increased Jewish immigration and settlement.

On the nationalist front, Vladimir Jabotinsky opposed the gradualism of mainstream Zionists and founded the militant Revisionist Party in 1925. He ruled out "a willing agreement between us and the Arabs", and sought an armed "wall of iron" to attain both sides of the Jordan as *Eretz Yisrael* (Greater Israel), a self-governing Jewish state with a Jewish majority.

In 1929 the Jewish Agency, authorized in the instrument of mandate seven years earlier, was formed. That same year the various socialist Zionist forces formed a powerful coalition under the umbrella of *Mapai*. The dynamic young David Ben-Gurion became their chairman and won control of the World Zionist Executive in 1933, giving him access to its large financial resources. *Mapai* (which dominated the *Histadrut*) believed in industrial progress but also in the sanctity of labouring on the soil, a new non-intellectual model for Jewish identity. This latter ideal was practised by the kibbutz movement of collective settlements founded in 1909—though sometimes at the expense of evicted Arab tenant farmers.

The concept of Palestine as a haven for persecuted Jewry grew. Between 1918 and 1932 125,000 Jews poured into the land, many fleeing renewed pogroms in a Russia racked by civil war and revolution. Many religious Jews, however, resisted Zionism. They saw a secular return to Zion as sacreligious, and preferred to wait until the Messiah would lead them as prophesied in the scriptures. Palestine's Chief Rabbi, Abraham Isaac Kook, nonetheless saw the atheist Jewish pioneers as part of the redemption plan. Where the

Arabs fitted into the plan was less clear. Writing in 1925, Weizmann said: "Six hundred thousand Arabs live there who . . . have exactly the same rights to their homes as we have to our National Home. Palestine," he added, "is not Rhodesia".

JEWISH-ARAB POLARIZATION, 1930–1939

Riots in 1929 in Jerusalem and the persecution of Jews in Europe after Hitler's rise to power in 1933 heralded a new and more violent stage of the Palestine dispute.

Palestinian Arabs were encouraged by Transjordan's independence from Britain in 1928, and Iraq's in 1932. Britain had already ended its Egyptian protectorate in 1922; in 1936 she limited her presence there to a Suez Canal garrison. In Palestine Britain was now caught between Jewish and Arab demands, and found it increasingly difficult to satisfy both sides.

Anger at Jewish immigration grew among Arabs. In August 1929 Haj Amin and the Supreme Moslem Council accused Jews of trying to "take over" Moslem sites near the old Jerusalem Temple Wall. Serious riots broke out after a Jewish demonstration at the Wailing Wall. In all 133 Jews and 116 Arabs died here and in Safed and Hebron, site of a religious Jewish settlement near the tomb of Abraham. A British commission blamed Zionist "provocation", and in October 1930 a White Paper from Colonial Secretary Lord Passfield proposed restrictions on Jewish immigration and land purchase. Prime Minister Ramsay MacDonald rejected this, however, which infuriated the *mufti*.

Britain's inability to curb the violence prompted the Jews to expand the *Hagana* in 1929, with the aim of training and arming all fit Jewish males in Palestine. It also provided military cover for "illegal" Jewish immigration, which increased after the Nazis came to power in Germany. While official British forces opposed the *Hagana*, some British (notably Captain Orde Wingate) sympathized with the Zionist cause. In 1936 Wingate trained and armed 3,000 Jewish authorized guards. That year the Revisionists and their *Betar* youth group, impatient with *Hagana*'s caution and uncomfortable with its socialist orientation, formed the *Irgun Zvai Leumi* defence organization.

In 1931 Izz e-Din al-Qassam organized the first *fedayeen* (Arab guerillas) and led them in attacks on Jewish settlements, and was leader of the

Palestine Mandatory government from 1933, till he died in a raid in November 1935. The four main Palestinian Arab parties temporarily ceased their in-fighting to form in April 1936 an Arab Higher Committee to oppose Jewish settlement. *Fedayeen* and *Irgun* clashes grew in intensity, and Britain declared a state of emergency (the initial *Hagana* response was one of "self-restraint").

In response the Higher Committee called for a general strike by Arabs, but six months later called it off when the moderate parties withdrew support, partially due to pressure from neighbouring Arab states. Haj Amin did not comply and the revolt continued, by now claiming the lives of many British soldiers. The British government sent Lord Peel to try to end the friction and meet the demands of the conflicting communities. In 1937 the Peel Commission recommended partition of the country into Arab and Jewish states. Arab Palestine was to rule over 85 per cent of the land; Jewish Palestine was to consist of the Galilee and a coastal strip; the Holy Cities of Jerusalem, Safed, Hebron and Shiloh would be under a special international mandate. The Zionist Congress (though not the Revisionists) reluctantly accepted the plan, but the Arab Higher Committee and Arab states rejected it. The latter's counter-proposal was to end the mandate and set up an independent majority-ruled Palestine. Meanwhile the national mass uprising continued till 1939, costing the lives of 517 Jews, over 3,000 Arabs and 150 British police and officials. Six thousand Arabs were imprisoned and 110 executed.

Faced with deadlock and an imminent world war, Britain dropped the partition plan in 1939 but continued to negotiate with the Arab Higher Committee which they had earlier banned (Haj Amin had fled to Lebanon). A new White Paper suggested restricting Jewish immigration to 75,000 over five years, pending Arab approval; prohibiting Jewish land purchases in 90 per cent of the land; and promised an independent Palestine within 10 years. Zionist groups were apalled in the face of the threat to European Jewry; some began new acts of terror against the British presence. Meanwhile, although the Palestinian National Defence Party accepted the White Paper, Husseini's Higher Committee rejected it because it did not mention a single unitary Palestinian state, and started forging closer ties with Nazi Germany. A virtual civil war ensued between these two Palestinian factions, resulting in thousands of casualties.

THE ROAD TO INDEPENDENCE, 1939–1948

Reacting to the unprecedented Nazi persecution of Jews, fully 225,000 Jews had left Germany and East and Central Europe for Palestine between 1933 and 1939, pushing the Jewish population to 445,000 by the eve of the war (30 per cent of the total).

In 1939 World War Two broke out, and 100,000 Palestinian Jews volunteered to serve with the British against the Nazi threat. In 1941 Palmach broke away from the *Hagana* to assist in this. Intercommunal strife abated during the war. Despite their North African conquests, the Germans never reached Palestine. By the war's end, six million European Jews had lost their lives in the Nazi Final Solution, or Holocaust.

Even so, Britain kept rigorously to the 1939 restrictions on immigration, letting in just 4,200 Jews in 1942. In February 1940 they banned Jewish land purchases in two thirds of the territory and restricted purchases in the remainder. But Arab frontline states suspected Britain was secretly helping the Jews create their own state, and in March 1945 formed the Arab League to block it. While "sympathizing" with Jewish suffering in the Holocaust, it rejected as "arbitrary and unjust . . . the wish to resolve the (Jewish question) by another injustice of which the Arabs of Palestine . . . would be the victims".

In May 1942 Ben-Gurion held a Zionist Congress in New York. From it emerged the "Biltmore Programme" which for the first time officially committed the Zionist movement to a Jewish state, attainable by military means if necessary; and called for an end to co-operation with Britain. When the war ended in 1945 Jewish anger turned against the Mandate. Zionists smuggled in camp survivors and arms, largely from the new Communist states. In November 1944 the Stern Gang (an offshoot of *Irgun*) assassinated Lord Moyne, British High Commissioner to Egypt, in Cairo. In 1946 they blew up the King David Hotel in Jerusalem, killing 91 people. Two British army sergeants were captured and hanged in reprisal for the execution of convicted Jewish guerrillas. Though the *Hagana* and Jewish Agency condemned these actions, they helped persuade Britain to leave Palestine.

In February 1947, after various proposed partition plans had failed in the face of Arab insistence on a unitary state, Britain referred the Palestine question to the newly formed United Nations. A Special Committee (UNSCOP) drew up a new partition plan: it called for (i) a Jewish state in three linking segments, eastern Galilee in the north, the coastal plain from Haifa to Rehovot in the south, and the Negev desert; (ii) an Arab state, made up of western Galilee, central Palestine, a southern littoral bordering Egypt, and the port of Jaffa; (iii) an international zone in Jerusalem and Bethlehem; and (iv) economic union between all regions.

In the aftermath of the discovery of the Nazi concentration camps, the United Nations General Assembly voted by 33 to 13 in favour of the plan on Nov. 29, 1947, thus giving legitimacy to the first Jewish state in 1,900 years. Despite growing mutual antipathy, both the USA and USSR voted for the proposal. The Jews of Palestine accepted the proposal, although it gave them less than half the land they claimed. Arab states and Palestinian Arabs, however, rejected the vote which they said contravened the UN Charter. Only the Marxist Palestine National League considered compromise.

In December 1947 Britain announced that it would relinquish its mandate in five months' time. On Jan. 12, 1948, the Jewish Agency and Jewish National Council announced plans for a provisional government. Meanwhile violence escalated. In February an Arab bomb killed 55 Jews in Jerusalem; in March the Jewish Agency offices were blown up and in retaliation *Hagana* took the port of Haifa at the cost of 400 lives and attacked Jaffa; in April *Irgun* killed 254 unarmed Arabs in Deir Yassin; then Arab forces killed 40 Jewish doctors and nurses; on May 12 another 100 Jews died at Kfar Etzion.

ISRAELI VICTORY, PALESTINIAN EXILE

On May 14, hours before the end of the Mandate, the State of Israel was proclaimed in Tel Aviv. US President Truman had appealed for a temporary UN trusteeship plan, but when Zionists ignored him and opted for full statehood, he recognized the provisional government. The Declaration of Independence called for unlimited Jewish immigration "to (fulfil) the dreams of generations for the redemption of Israel".

It also committed the new state to the United Nations Charter, and invited Israeli Arabs to "play their part in the development of the state on the basis of full and equal citizenship". To the Arab states it said: "We extend the hand of peace and neighbourliness . . . and invite them to co-operate with us for the common good of all." Hours after the Declaration forces from Egypt, Transjordan, Syria, Iraq and Lebanon invaded the new state. The Arab League said its aim was to restore "peace, security and the rule of law" so that "the lawful inhabitants of Palestine, by virtue of their absolute sovereignty . . . (could establish) a unitary independent Palestine state, in accordance with democratic principles." They assured "minorities" of "guarantees recognized in democratic constitutional countries".

The USA, USSR and UN Security Council promptly condemned the invasion as an act of aggression. Within two weeks Israel launched a counter-offensive, holding on to the land promised by the UN and adding areas of Galilee, Negev and Jaffa, as well as a strip linking the coastal plain with west Jerusalem. Poor co-ordination between League forces and the Liberation Army under Fawzi el Kaukji partially accounts for their failure. By early 1949 the war was over; Israel controlled two-thirds of Palestinian territory, and signed armistices with the defeated parties. East Jerusalem (the Old City, Temple Mount and Jewish Quarter) plus the West Bank came under Jordanian jurisdiction, and the Gaza Strip under Egyptian rule.

At least one per cent of the Jewish population (more than 6,000 people) lost their lives in the war; no official Arab casualty figures were released. The war not only formed the Jewish state, it also changed the demography of the region. Both sides in the dispute give evidence that the other forced the Palestinians out. An estimated 780,000 Palestinian Arabs were displaced from their homes; 150,000 remained in Israel. But now most Israelis (660,000) were Jews—for the first time in 1,900 years forming a majority in their own Jewish state.

INDEPENDENCE AND WAR

As the storm clouds of war dispersed, the Jewish people looked at what they had created. At last they were a majority in the land of Israel. The shadow state apparatus of the Mandate—army, industry, legal system, schools and universities—were the bedrock for a new state, with the Star of David as its national flag. Herzl's dream of a "normal" Jewish condition was a reality. At times, however, this required abnormal changes: European names were Hebraized, Hebrew was adopted as the national language, British legal mores combined with a quasi-Marxist industrial-labour complex and Talmudic laws. Young men were compelled to do military service. The army became a source of leading politicians (Dayan, Rabin, Eshkol, Yadin, Sharon).

Indeed, the army's role was magnified by the ever-present outside threat, and it unified a nation which threatened to split over deep ideological divisions. In 1933 right-wing Revisionists had murdered a leading Socialist Zionist, Chaim Arlosoroff. In 1948 *Irgun* was meant to merge with the *Hagana*, but Menachem Begin led his arms ship *Altalena* into Haifa and did not surrender until fired on by army chief Eshkol.

David Ben-Gurion was the first Prime Minister, heading a Labour government (he was to rule, except for two years, till 1964); Chaim Weizmann was President. Many saw Israel as a miracle following the nightmare of the Nazi Holocaust; but for the displaced Palestinians, their troubles were just beginning.

Much has been written about how they got into that predicament. Arabs claim they fled fearing massacres like that of Deir Yassin. Menachem Begin is on record as saying: "The massacre was not only justified, but there would not have been a state of Israel without the victory of Deir Yassin". Ben Gurion, however, sent an apology on behalf of the Jewish Agency to King Abdullah of Transjordan. Other Arabs say Jewish troops expelled Palestinians in order to achieve the Jewish majority. Israelis claim Arab Higher Executive and League broadcasts ordered the people to leave, until such time as the "Zionist entity" was destroyed. Most Palestinians thus believed their absence would be a short one. Israelis point to appeals by the Jewish mayor and unions of Haifa and elsewhere, calling on Arabs to stay (in the event Arab broadcasts warned that Arabs who stayed in Haifa and accepted Jewish protection would be regarded as renegades, and only 6,000 of the original population of 62,000 stayed).

It is true that expulsion was never the official policy of the Zionists, but recent documents show that some Israeli military commanders used threats to force out Palestinian civilians. Richer Palestinian families (notables, officials and professionals) left when war broke out; many of the now leaderless masses followed them. While the better educated Palestinians made new lives for themselves in the capitals of the Arab world, the less fortunate stayed in refugee camps. As of June 30, 1986, the number of refugees registered with the UN Relief and Works Agency for Palestine Refugees (UNRWA) totalled 2,145,794. Of these, 749,235 are in camps; the largest and most densely populated are found in the Gaza Strip.

The Arab states' sense of humiliation at their loss in the 1948–49 war found voice in persecution of their own Jewish communities. As a result many Arabic-speaking Sephardic Jews fled to Israel, adding a new flavour to the Jewish State. Between 1948 and 1964, Israel gained 123,000 new citizens from Iraq, 120,000 from Morocco, 75,000 from Egypt, 48,000 from Yemen, and 35,000 from Libya. The 1967 war brought in thousands more. Israeli officials depict this influx as a refugee problem, counterbalancing the departure of Palestinians. In Zionist eyes the incoming of Jewish people fulfilled the biblical prophecies, though in this modern age new immigrants learnt Western skills from European Jews.

PEACE TALKS BREAK DOWN, 1948–1955

On Dec. 11, 1948, a UN Palestine Conciliation Commission was set up to solve the refugee problem and to get peace talks underway. By April of the following year, Israel, Egypt, Transjordan and Syria signed a protocol in Lausanne agreeing on the 1947 UN partition plan as a "basis for discussion". Talks soon broke down—Israel wanted the refugee problem to be dealt with as part of a general peace settlement, while the Arabs wanted the problem solved before any peace deal.

Positions hardened on both sides. On Jan. 23, 1950, the Israeli *Knesset*

(Parliament) declared West Jerusalem as the capital. On April 24 the Jordanian Parliament incorporated the West Bank and East Jerusalem (intended as the basis of an Arab Palestine) into the Hashemite Kingdom. Both actions contravened the UN partition plan, by now widely seen as null and void, and were condemned by Palestinians as a betrayal of their rights.

On May 25, 1950, Britain, France and the USA jointly stated their opposition to the violation of frontiers or 1949 armistice lines, and committed themselves to preventing an arms race in the region. All the bordering Arab states remained in a state of war with Israel; Egypt denied Israel use of the Suez Canal, and promoted Palestinian *Fedayeen* attacks on the new state from Gaza, which they administered. In 1953 Egypt started restricting Israeli sea-borne trade through the Straits of Tiran at the mouth of the Gulf of Aqaba.

The first Arab-Israeli war had had a profound effect on the political life of Egypt and Jordan. King Abdullah of Transjordan was assassinated in 1951 by one of the Palestinians who made up more than half his population. He was succeeded by his grandson, Hussein, who still rules today. Shamed by defeat, Egypt's King Farouk was overthrown by a military junta. In 1954 the radical young colonel Gamal Abdal Nasser took over, launching Egypt on a course of socialism fused with pan-Arab nationalism. He began severing ties with Western powers, and signed an arms deal with Communist Czechoslovakia in September 1955. In February 1956 Israel raided the Qilqilya camp in Gaza, in retaliation for *Fedayeen* raids promoted by Egypt. Raids and counter-raids escalated, and Israel planned for war.

THE SUEZ CANAL WAR AND AFTERMATH, 1956–1963

Meanwhile, the Canal Zone had become a source of conflict between Egypt and the Suez Canal Company run by Britain and France. Britain withdrew forces from the Zone in a 1954 treaty with Egypt, but in July 1956, after Britain denied finance for the Aswan Dam project, Nasser nationalized the Canal Company. Britain, France and Israel planned a secret attack on Egypt in October, the former to regain the canal, the latter to secure more defensible borders. None of them consulted the USA, who harboured its own ambitions for Middle Eastern influence and saw British and French colonial interests there as a diversion.

Israel attacked Egyptian positions in Gaza and the Sinai on Oct. 29; Britain and France then issued ultimatums to both sides to withdraw from the Canal. When Egypt refused, Anglo–French paratroopers and commandos occupied the Canal Zone. Israel took the opportunity to overrun the Sinai.

By Nov. 6, however, joint American and Soviet pressure at the UN Security Council forced Britain to accept a ceasefire and evacuate her troops. A UN Emergency Force (UNEF) took their place. Israel withdrew from the Sinai, but kept forces in Gaza and Eilat till March 1957, assured that the UNEF would prevent *Fedayeen* incursions, and that Israel could enjoy free sea passage in the Gulf of Aqaba.

The three main consequences of the brief Suez war were: i) diminution of Britain's role in the region; ii) increasing ties between the Soviet Union and the radical Arab states of Egypt, Syria and Iraq; and iii) a growing US role in the region, backing Israel and conservative Arab states, partly to counter the Soviet Union's influence.

From the Israeli–Palestinian perspective, the war changed little. Israel demonstrated its military prowess, but its forced withdrawal from the Sinai showed up its diplomatic weakness and left her with vulnerable borders. Furthermore, Syria still bombarded settlements from the Golan Heights and only 10 miles separated Israel from the Jordanian West Bank and the Mediterranean Sea. Palestinians realized that Egyptian patronage alone could not help win back lost lands.

The UNEF presence temporarily quelled incidents in Gaza, though new clashes took place between Israel and Jordan over the demilitarized zone in Jerusalem in 1957 and 1958. Israel and Syria clashed over the Galilee, starting in 1957 and reaching a pinnacle in 1963.

Other disputes exacerbated the Arab–Israeli conflict—after 1959 Egypt began a new blockade of Israeli trade through the Suez Canal; Jordan, Lebanon and Syria quarrelled with Israel over distribution of the waters of the Jordan River. In 1964 Arab heads of state met in Cairo and resolved to limit water supply to Israel (though in practice this was hard to achieve).

THE FOUNDATION OF THE PLO AND THE LEAD-UP TO WAR, 1964–1967

None of these disputes, however, touched on the Palestinian populace directly. In September 1948 Haj Amin had set up a "Government of All Palestine" in exile under Egyptian auspices, but this had little credibility and was soon dissolved. Palestinian frustration was partially assuaged by the January 1964 Arab summit decision to set up a Palestine National Council (PNC), or parliament-in-exile. Ahmad Shukairy, a lawyer born in Acre, was its first President. The PNC consisted of 422 representatives, more than half from Jordan. At its first session, held in Jordanian-occupied Jerusalem in June 1964, the PNC established the Palestine Liberation Organisation (PLO) as the armed wing of their struggle to "regain the land".

The 33-article Palestine National Charter (or "Covenant") was adopted as a statement of aims. Among these were: the indivisibility of Palestine and the legal rights of the Palestinian people to "liberate it . . . entirely of their own accord" (articles 1, 2 and 3); a rejection of the 1947 Partition, the Balfour Declaration and "the claims of historical or religious ties of Jews with Palestine" (articles 19 and 20); a declaration that "armed struggle is the only way to liberate Palestine" (article 9) and rejection of a solution falling short of this.

Palestine was to be an "indivisible part of the Arab homeland", and the PNC called on the support of all progressive people in the world. However, according to article 12, at this stage Palestinian identity had to be safeguarded vis-à-vis any broader Arab identity. Palestinians were defined as Arab nationals of pre-1947 Palestine and their descendants, and Jews resident in Palestine before the "Zionist invasion". Though the Charter promised freedom of worship to all, Zionism was deemed "racist and fanatic in its nature, aggressive, expansionist and colonial in its aims and fascist in its methods"; so the fate of Israeli Jews seemed precarious.

Soon, however, other *Fedayeen* groups arose to contest the mainstream PLO's claim to represent all Palestinians. Prominent among these was Yasser Arafat's *Al-Fatah* (Victory), which came to public notice after a New Year's Day raid on Israeli water pipes in 1965. There were a further 34 *Fatah* raids that year, mostly from Jordan, though *Fatah* was backed by Syria. The period that ensued has been characterized as pro-Syrian PLO affiliates forcing the hand of Shukairy and his mentor, Nasser. Using the Voice of Palestine radio station, Shukairy attacked King Hussein's authority over his Palestinian subjects in Jordan. The quarrel resulted in Jordan breaking relations with the PLO in July 1966. On Nov. 13, after repeated *Fedayeen* raids, Israel attacked the West Bank village of Samu.

Rioting broke out as Palestinians and Iraq, Syria and Egypt demanded that Jordan allow a "united Arab force" to be stationed in the West Bank. In January 1967 the PLO offices in Jerusalem were shut down and moved to Cairo. After repeated air and ground clashes between Israel and Syria, Israeli Prime Minister, Levi Eshkol, warned on May 14 of full-scale war if guerrilla incursions continued. Egypt, Syria and Jordan announced states of emergency and full mobilization. On May 19 the United Nations bowed to Nasser's pressure and withdrew the UNEF forces from the Sinai.

The PLO placed its forces under the commands of Egypt, Syria and Iraq, and Nasser closed the Gulf of Aqaba to Israeli shipping. Israeli Foreign Minister Abba Eban told the UN it would break the blockade by force if necessary. Egypt and Jordan signed a joint defence pact, and warned other nations against supporting Israel; Iraqi forces moved through Jordan towards Israel. Early on the morning of June 5, Israel launched a pre-emptive strike on Egyptian airfields; Jordanian troops moved against Israel. Thus began the Six Day War.

ISRAEL GAINS NEW TERRITORIES, 1967–68

The war was one of the shortest on record, but the effects were profound. By June 10, Israel had i) captured the Gaza Strip and the entire Sinai peninsula up to the Suez Canal; ii) gained control of East Jerusalem (including the Old City) and overrun all Jordanian land west of the River Jordan; and iii) captured the Golan Heights in the north from Syria. Israeli forces now occupied more than three times as much territory as they did post-1948 (the new territories covered 70,000 sq km, as opposed to 20,000 sq km before).

In short, it was a total victory for Israel. They lost 766 troops compared to 10,000 for Egypt and 6,000 for Jordan. Most significantly, Israel now ruled four times as many Palestinians as they did before the war. Although 200,000 fled from the West Bank during the fighting, some 600,000 remained there, as did a further 300,000 in the Gaza Strip.

Israeli leaders immediately offered negotiations, though rejected demands by the USSR and others to return to 1949 armistice lines. Speaking at a special UN General Assembly session, Eban called for a "new future in the Middle East (of) permanent peace . . . The Arab states can no longer be permitted to recognize Israel's existence only for the purpose of plotting its elimination. They have come face to face with us in conflict. Now let them come face to face with us in peace . . .".

The Arab world, however, stunned by the magnitude of their defeat, resolved not to negotiate with Israel. King Hussein spurned Eban's offer at the UN, and blamed Israel for the war. An Arab summit at Khartoum in August committed itself to "make no peace with Israel, for the sake of the rights of the Palestinian people in their homeland".

On Nov. 22 the UN Security Council unanimously adopted Resolution 242 proposed by Britain, which stressed "the inadmissibility of the acquisition of territory by war and the need to work for a just and lasting peace in which every state in the area can live in security." It demanded: i) Israeli withdrawal from occupied territories; ii) mutual respect for the sovereignty of all states in the area within secure boundaries; iii) freedom of navigation in international waterways; iv) a just settlement of the refugee problem; and v) demilitarized zones.

Both Israel and the frontline Arab states (except Syria) accepted the Resolution, though disagreed over the definition of Israeli withdrawal. The PLO rejected the Resolution as it made no mention of Palestinian national rights. Indeed, one practical effect of the war was a sidestepping of the Palestinian issue, as Arab states sought first to regain their own lost land. One casualty of the war was Shukairy, deposed as PLO head in December 1967.

Israel did not annex her new territories, with the exception of a "reunited" Jerusalem which was subsequently declared the capital. The UN General Assembly condemned this by 99 votes to none, with 20 abstentions. In July the Cabinet considered Brigadier Yigal Allon's plan to incorporate a largely uninhabited 30 per cent of the West Bank and all of Gaza, for security reasons.

But a new breed of orthodox Jewish Zionists saw settlement as a God-given duty, as to them this area was Judaea and Samaria—with Gaza, part of *Eretz Yisrael*. In August 1967 they formed the Land of Israel Movement, an extra-party pressure group, and in 1973 the *Gush Emunim* (Bloc of the Faithful), finding allies among "hawks" in the right-wing opposition *Likud* Party. Considering the same land was seen by Arabs as historical Palestine, the stage was set for an intensification of the Arab–Israeli dispute.

"ATTRITION" AND THE YOM KIPPUR WAR, 1969–1973

In the aftermath of the Six Day War Arafat's *Fedayeen* tried to regain the initiative by raids on Israeli installations within the occupied territories. After a fierce battle at Karameh on the West Bank in March 1968, when the PLO fighters allegedly held the Israeli troops at bay, Arafat's prestige rose. He led the redrafting of the PNC Charter in July 1968, which rejected political solutions; and in February 1969 was voted chairman of the PLO. Other more left-wing Palestinians also rejoined the PLO, notably groups led by Georges Habash, Ahmed Jabril and Nayef Hawatmeh, and the pro-Syrian *Saiqa* movement. It was their influence which led to the final schism with Jordan.

Meanwhile a "War of Attrition" began with Israel, centred around the Suez Canal and costing 177 Israeli lives and 681 *Fedayeen* casualties in 1968.

By the end of June 1972 more Israelis had died in action than in the Six Day War. In Jordan the *Fedayeen* became increasingly assertive, till King Hussein unleashed his bedouin troops on them in the 11-day "Black September" conflict in 1970. By summer 1971 all *Fedayeen* were expelled from the Kingdom and fled to Syria and Lebanon. In revenge *Fedayeen* killed the Jordanian premier, Wasfi al-Tal.

By September 1975 Israel had withdrawn a further 40 kilometres in the Sinai and vacated the Abu Rideis oilfields, creating a UN demilitarized buffer zone. Both sides promised to refrain from use of force, and non-military cargoes en route to Israel could again travel the canal. In return the USA promised i) to help Israel militarily and economically, ii) to consult with her over a Geneva peace conference and general Middle East settlement and iii) not to deal with a PLO under its "present orientation".

PLO AND "INTERNATIONAL TERRORISM", 1973–77

The PLO was superficially united behind Arafat and his *Fatah* forces, but under the surface he faced dissent from a strong Rejection Front which spurned any political solution of the Palestinian question. While "moderates" considered plans for a "partial" Palestinian state on the West Bank and Gaza, possibly in federation with Jordan, thus tacitly recognizing the state of Israel, "radicals" favoured armed struggle to conquer all of historical Palestine. Grafted onto this fundamental division were further disputes over the political orientation of a future Palestine (secular or Muslim, democratic or military, capitalist or socialist) and disputes over Arafat's leadership.

Acts of terror by minority factions like the Popular Front for the Liberation of Palestine (PFLP), sanctioned to varying degrees by PLO mainliners, kept the Palestinian cause in the news. Among these were: attacks led by Leila Khaled, of Ahmed Jabril's PFLP-General Command, on a Swiss airliner (47 killed) and an Israeli schoolbus (12 killed) in 1970; hijackings by Georges Habash's PFLP in 1969 and 1970, and a massacre at Lod airport in Israel in 1972; Black September's killing of 11 Israeli athletes at the Munich Olympic Games in 1972; and Hawatmeh's Democratic Front for the Liberation of Palestine's attack on Maalot in northern Israel in 1974, in which 20 schoolchildren were killed.

Golda Meir had succeeded the late Levi Eshkol as Israel's Premier on March 17, 1969. She rejected a French plan for superpower mediation and a peace proposal from King Hussein of Jordan. Egypt's President Nasser died in September 1970, and was succeeded by Anwar Sadat, who swore to regain the lands lost in 1967. That same year Hafez al-Assad rose to power in Syria, and started arming *Fatah* guerrillas now based in southern Lebanon. Egypt and Israel signed a ceasefire in 1970, despite the breakdown of the US Rogers Plan to bring lasting peace. In 1971 Egypt signed a Friendship Treaty with USSR, giving her access to arms. Tensions rose in the region in 1973 with Israel's downing of a Libyan airliner over the Sinai, killing 74 in February; and a fierce Syrian–Israeli air battle over Lebanon in September. This, plus hijackings by PLO factions and escalating violence in Lebanon, paved the way for another war.

On Oct. 6, 1973 Egyptian and Syrian forces attacked Israel on Yom Kippur, the holiest day of the Jewish year. Caught unawares, Israel suffered initial losses but fought back to regain equity by the time the ceasefire was agreed on Oct. 24. Israel lost 2,400 troops and 1,300 square kilometres of the Sinai.

STEPS TOWARDS "THE PEACE OPTION", 1974–1977

The Yom Kippur War changed the political dispensation in the region. Despite failing to regain more than a fraction of the Sinai, Egyptian and Arab League honour was restored, giving Sadat the confidence to negotiate from a position of strength. Israel, by contrast, was shocked by its brush with defeat. Moshe Dayan, the hero of the 1967 war, was forced to resign as Defence Minister, together with Premier Golda Meir in April 1974. Right-wing elements claimed that more than ever tighter security in the territories was now essential to safeguard the state. The USA and USSR had pumped vast amounts of arms into Israel and the Arab states respectively, and later revealed how close the war had come to escalating into an international conflict. Although Palestinians again played a minimal role in the war, the PLO's prestige rose in Arab eyes. On Oct. 29, 1974 an Arab League summit in Rabat (including an initially recalcitrant Jordan) recognized it as sole representative of the Palestinian people.

The two years that followed the war saw new and apparently contradictory trends emerge: i) the willingness of Arab states to negotiate disengagement agreements with Israel; ii) Arab use of the "oil weapon" to punish pro-Israeli Western states; and iii) increased Palestinian "terrorism". Arab states restricted the flow of oil to most Western nations, thus forcing the price to quadruple and sparking off a worldwide economic crisis. Oil, rather than appeals to Palestinian rights, proved a stronger bargaining counter at this stage.

On Oct. 22, 1973 the UN Security Council passed the first ceasefire resolution, 338, calling for the implementation of 242 and the creation of a new UNEF to be deployed on the Suez Front in November. The formal signing of a ceasefire at "Kilometre 101" between Israel and Egypt was the first such conclusive agreement since the armistice of 1949. Egypt wanted Israeli troops off her soil (Israel had gained control of the town of Suez and some 1,300 square kilometres west of the canal). US Secretary of State Henry Kissinger began intense "shuttle diplomacy" to achieve peace.

A joint USA–USSR attempt to get Egypt, Syria, Jordan and Israel to agree to a peace conference failed on Jan. 9, 1974 when Syria refused to join (the PLO had not been invited). Disengagement talks, however, continued, and on Jan. 18 Egypt gained control of both sides of the canal. Israel held on to the strategic Mitla and Giddi passes and the Straits of Tiran, plus most of the peninsula. In May Israel withdrew from land she had captured from Syria in the war, and returned the town of Quneitra, while holding on to the strategic Golan Heights.

In April 1973 Israeli commandos of *Mossad* (the intelligence service) attacked the Black September headquarters in Beirut. *Fatah* condemned terrorist action outside the Middle East, but continued her own raids against Israel, notably with a seaborne attack on Tel Aviv in June 1975 which claimed 18 lives.

The ostensible reason for most terrorist action was the release of Palestinians held in detention by Israel. Often the terrorist cells consisted of Palestinians aided by European or Japanese radicals. A new spate of incidents began in 1975 and 1976: the seizure of Egypt's ambassador to Spain in September 1975 and of politicians from the Organization of Petroleum Exporting Countries (OPEC) in Vienna in December; the attack on an Egyptian airliner at Beirut airport on Oct. 4, 1975; the hijacking of an Air France airliner to Entebbe, Uganda, in June 1976; the grenade attack on an Israeli airliner at Istanbul on Aug. 11; the hijacking of a Dutch airliner on Sept. 4; and an abortive attack on the Intercontinental Hotel in Amman, when seven died. There was also a spate of assassinations of PLO and Arab leaders: PLO representative Mahmoud Selah in Paris on Jan. 3, 1977; former North Yemen Premier Hajri on April 10, 1978; former Iraqi Premier Col. al Nayef on July 9, 1978, and Said Hammami, PLO representative in Britain, on Jan. 4, 1978, all in London. The Abu Nidal group was suspected, though PLO officials often blamed Israeli intelligence.

THE PLO'S DIPLOMATIC OFFENSIVE: 1974–77

After Israel and Jordan cleared their areas of PLO men, the guerrillas concentrated on raids from Lebanon. In 1974 the Melkart Agreement reinforced the 1969 Cairo Agreement, guaranteeing Lebanese state authority under Syrian auspices but also the PLO's right to keep an armed presence in the south (nicknamed "Fatahland"). Full-scale Lebanese civil war broke out in 1975; PLO units began siding with leftist Druze and Moslems against Christian forces.

The Rabat conference of Arab states in October 1974 effectively deferred political decisions on the Palestinian issue to the PLO. In the UN 90 states had recognized the PLO as "legitimate representatives" of the Palestinians. The UN General Assembly voted by 72 to 14 to invite Yasser Arafat to address them on Nov. 13, 1974. In a now famous speech he claimed he wanted a "peaceful solution in Palestine's sacred land"—he bore "an olive branch in one hand and a freedom fighter's gun in the other", and twice warned the Assembly not to let the branch drop. Arafat equated Zionism with racism and reminded the Assembly of their condemnations of Israel's "military aggression", though never mentioned Resolution 242. He claimed his enemy was Zionism and not Judaism, though this did little to assuage Israelis who noted rising anti-Jewish feelings in Arab states. Israel's UN representative retorted that "Jordan is Palestine" and vowed to "pursue the murderers of the PLO and destroy their bases".

The PNC had met in June, re-elected Arafat as PLO chairman and for the first time accepted as many independents on the executive committee as guerrilla leaders. But Arafat's peace overtures and willingness to accept Arab–Israeli disengagement agreements were rejected by the PFLP and others who left the PLO executive committee in September 1974 to form a Rejection Front on Oct. 14. On Nov. 16 Said Hammami, London representative of the PLO, wrote in the London *Times* for the first time of a need for a mini-state of Palestine consisting of the West Bank and Gaza, possibly as a "first step" to a fully secular Palestine in all of the land. In effect, this recognized the Israeli state in pre-1967 borders, and marked a belated Palestinian return to the partition plan they had rejected in 1947 and earlier. Although his view was repudiated by PLO headquarters, it was the view of a minority in the PLO.

On April 12 that year municipal elections were held in the West Bank in accordance with Jordanian law, the first large poll there since 1972. (Israeli Arabs voted in general elections, and two Arabs sat in the *Knesset*, but West Bank and Gaza Palestinians had no vote). The result was a victory for National

Bloc candidates, largely pro-PLO and *Rakah* (New Communist). On a 71 per cent turnout, the Bloc won most of the 148 seats which changed hands, out of a total of 205 at issue. They now controlled Nablus, Hebron and Ramallah, but lost to pro-Jordanian candidates in Jericho and Bethlehem.

UNREST ON THE WEST BANK, 1975–1977

The question of Jewish settlements was a major issue in the election. Until now, most unrest had taken place in Gaza, where most of the population lived in refugee camps. Now in 1975 secret buying of West Bank land by the Israel Lands Authority had prompted unrest, which intensified when *Gush Emunim* extremists tried to settle at Sebastia in December 1975 and Kafr Qaddum in January 1976. Bombs exploded in Jerusalem in April and May, and Palestinians declared a general strike in Nablus. Several died as Israeli troops tried to contain demonstrations. Many West Bank mayors resigned in protest. On Oct. 2 and 3 Moslems and Jews in Hebron desecrated each others' sacred scrolls, and a curfew was declared. In 1975 a total of 144 people died or were wounded in attacks in Jerusalem.

In April 1975 Defence Minister Shimon Peres had announced five new West Bank settlements to join the present 16, calling them "the country's defence line", but now he and the Cabinet condemned *Gush Emunim* for provoking local Palestinians. The rest of the blame fell on the PLO, especially after two sabotage incidents in Tel Aviv in May. In October a *Fatah* cell leader was sentenced for a plot to murder "collaborators". But *Fatah* itself became a target for attack by militant groups like the Abu Nidal Group. Within Israel proper, a Cabinet plan to expropriate Arab land in the Galilee on Feb. 29, 1976 prompted the Communist Mayor of Nazareth, Tewfik Zayyad, to call a general strike. Six more died in unrest on March 30, an incident since known as "Land Day", and as such commemorated annually by Palestinians. Six months later a report by the Galilee commissioner calling for curbs on Arab population growth and work rights was leaked. Though condemned by Foreign Minister Allon, it prompted widespread strikes. More broke out on Dec. 15 after mayors protested against a new Israeli tax, and these were followed by hunger-strikes in overcrowded prisons. Hundreds of suspected *Fatah* members were arrested.

Israel's policy on the territories remained ambiguous. In 1973 Dayan had sought to extend the Allon Plan of 1967 by integrated road and electricity networks in the area, thus preventing a "repartition" of the "Land of Israel". Indeed, improved irrigation and mechanization by Israel had boosted farm production in the territories by 10 per cent a year since 1968; Israel founded the Bir Zeit University near Ramallah in 1972, and by 1976 there were 229,000 pupils at school in the West Bank and 140,000 in Gaza and Sinai; an "open bridges" policy allowed Palestinians to visit relatives in neighbouring countries.

But overt political expression was banned by the military administration, a number of leaders were expelled and Jews took Arab land in occupied east Jerusalem. Of the 84 planned or extant settlements in the territories, half were on the Golan Heights; but by the end of 1976 the government authorized new ones in heavily populated Samaria. The UN Security Council (including the USA, which had previously used its veto) unanimously condemned such "demographic alterations" as having "no legal validity, and being a threat to peace". In 1976 and 1977 some 17,000 Palestinians left the West Bank. Nearly 60 per cent of the 1.34 million population of the territories were under 18.

POLITICAL CHANGE IN ISRAEL, 1974–77

The second Egyptian–Israeli disengagement treaty was implemented in February 1976, but attempts to revive the Geneva conference hit two stumbling blocks: i) Arab demands that Israel withdraw from all occupied territories; and ii) Israeli insistence that they would never talk with the PLO as long as the latter "totally denies Israel's right to exist".

There seemed little way out of this impasse. Israel continued the *de facto* integration of the West Bank and Gaza into the Israeli economy, and the PLO gave the lie to its peaceful proclamations by becoming ever more embroiled in the Lebanese civil war to Israel's north.

When Yitzhak Rabin took power in April 1974 from Golda Meir he faced a divided Labour party, though timely support from arch-rival Shimon Peres helped him form a government. The oil embargo and cost of rearming after the 1973 war, however, overstrained the economy and led to galloping inflation. The only respite in Israel's gloom was the commando rescue of hostages from a hijacked Air France airliner in Entebbe, Uganda, in July 1976. Rocked by financial scandal, Rabin resigned in April 1977 to be replaced by Peres. This bred widespread disenchantment among the electorate, and coupled with the effects of inflation and impatience over perceived international hostility to the Jewish state, made for a new right-wing mood on the eve of the general election in May 1977.

CAMP DAVID AND AFTER

LIKUD VICTORY IN THE ISRAELI ELECTIONS, 1977

Israel on the eve of the May 1977 general election was quite a different country from the state formed in 1948, and indeed from the nation facing war in June 1967. Her land mass was vastly bigger after the conquests of the Six Day War, and now encompassed the huge desert wilderness of the Sinai peninsula, plus the densely populated refugee camps and Palestinian villages of the Gaza Strip and the West Bank. Thanks largely to Jewish immigration from Arab lands, facilitated by the Law of Return whereby all Diaspora Jews could become Israeli citizens, her population had tripled in size since 1947. Native-born Israelis (nicknamed "Sabras") formed an ever-increasing percentage of the population.

Over the years Israel's political orientation had changed, from being a nominally non-aligned socialist state to a firm ally of the West, particularly of the USA. In part this reflected gratitude to American Jews for their generous donations. Israel's state defence expenditure was proportionately one of the highest in the world, and this produced a huge strain on the economy, causing massive inflation. The economy was still dominated by state industries, notably *Koor* and *Histradut* affiliates, run by older settlers from Europe who also controlled the government.

Since the foundation of the state, Israel had been governed by the Labour Alignment (now called *Ma'arach*) in coalition with smaller parties including the religious ones. On the far left were a smattering of Communist and pro-Palestinian MPs; but the chief opposition came from the right, and particularly from the *Likud* coalition led by the *Herut* party of Menachem Begin, a disciple of Vladimir Jabotinsky and former leader of the *Irgun*.

His party favoured freer enterprise combined with more settlements in the territories (or "Greater Israel" as *Likud* called it). Ironically, it was to be Begin and not his more liberal predecessors who achieved the first major peace settlement with the surrounding Arab world. In 1967 *Herut* had joined a Government of National Unity, but left in 1970 when the cabinet began talks with Arab states under UN auspices and considered territorial compromise. Since then Begin had opposed Labour bitterly for allegedly mismanaging the economy and not preparing the nation for the 1973 war. They appealed to Sephardic Jews who felt excluded by the Ashkenazic "establishment", and disputed Labour's tacit claim to be the natural government of Israel.

Likud won the 1977 election on May 18, and scored another coup in post-poll bargaining when (after acceding to changes in the law) they achieved the realignment of the National Religious Party (NRP) to the right-wing camp. Since 1967 the 15 per cent or so of the electorate who voted for religious parties began taking a more openly Zionist stance, backing the *Gush Emunim*, a group which favoured increased West Bank settlement. The alliance with *Likud* formalized this trend. The composition of Begin's cabinet reflected a more hawkish stance: Moshe Dayan was foreign minister; Gen. Ariel Sharon, founder of Israeli paratroops and Greater Israel protagonist, headed the Ministerial Settlement Committee; and Itzhak Shamir, former Stern Gang leader, was *Knesset* Speaker.

In July the new government sanctioned the building of three West Bank settlements, and warned that "renunciation of the smallest piece of the West Bank will lead inevitably to the creation of a Palestinian state which will . . . place the existence of Israel in danger and will endanger any chance of peace". Since capturing the area in the 1967 war, Israel had scarcely altered its Jordanian laws. But now her rulers explicitly proclaimed the land as Jewish by right. In ensuing years the so-called Green Line dividing Israel proper from the territories grew fainter as pipelines and roads integrated the two sectors economically, and Arabs streamed daily across the border to work in Israeli factories and on building sites. Israel nonetheless shunned outright annexation—it would be too controversial within Israel, and lose her Western backing and friends in the Diaspora. Most significantly, it would create a much larger Arab minority, with full citizenship rights, within the Jewish state and thereby threaten its identity.

SADAT IN JERUSALEM—PEACE TALKS BEGIN, 1977–1978

By approving the new settlements, Begin delivered a clear snub to the new US President, Jimmy Carter, who had called on Arab states to establish links with Israel, within the framework of a "homeland" for Palestinians, and "defensible" borders for Israel. His remarks were welcomed by Arafat but treated cautiously by Begin's predecessor, Rabin, whom he met in March 1977. In April Carter met Egypt's Anwar Sadat and Jordan's King Hussein. In various media interviews, Sadat mooted a Palestinian state "linked" with Jordan; Rabin's foreign minister Allon welcomed this apparent retreat from the concept of a PLO-ruled "third state" between Israel and Jordan. Sadat had broken off his Friendship Treaty with the USSR the previous March, but now faced food riots and needed a new ally. Israel in turn faced Palestinian demonstrations in Ramallah and Nablus on the West Bank.

For peace to be achieved both sides had to make concessions, but all indications revealed the opposite. Syria, who consistently opposed talks with Israel, started mending fences with Egypt and the PLO at the end of 1976. On March 12, 1977, Sadat said he would not allow a single inch of Arab land to remain under Israeli occupation. Then in a speech to the People's Assembly on Nov. 9, he announced that he was "ready to go to the *Knesset* (Israeli parliament) itself" to get the peace process going, and invited other Arab leaders to join him. Begin accepted his offer two days later, so that on Nov. 19–20 he became the first Arab leader ever to visit Israel. In the *Knesset* he stated that he accepted Israel's existence, but warned that no peace would last unless Israel withdrew from occupied territory and recognized the rights of Palestinians. On a triumphal return to Cairo, Sadat repeated his calls for peace talks involving the US and USSR.

On Dec. 25–26 Begin became the first Israeli leader to visit an Arab country when he held talks with Sadat in Ismailia. There he announced his plan for returning the Sinai to Egypt and for Palestinian "self-rule" in "Judea, Samaria and Gaza", involving the election of an Administrative Council responsible for economic and social affairs, but with security and public order remaining under Israeli control. The military administration would be abolished and residents could choose Israeli or Jordanian citizenship. Those who chose the former could settle in Israel but likewise Israelis could settle in the territories. Israel decided to "leave open" the question of sovereignty in the territories, and suggested a tripartite committee of Israel, Jordan and the Council to decide on the repatriation of Palestinian refugees from outside the area.

Most Arab states rejected Egypt's rapprochement with Israel. In December 1977, Egypt severed ties with Syria, Libya, Algeria and South Yemen, who had formed a "Steadfastness and Resistance Front", also known as the Tripoli bloc. The PLO saw it as an attempt to regain lost territory for Egypt while ignoring the interests of Palestinians. In January 1978 they rejected a call by Sadat and Carter for Palestinian participation in the peace process, and in March a Palestinian group killed 37 Israelis in a machine-gun attack in the north. In retaliation 7,000 Israeli troops invaded south Lebanon to seal the border against further raids, but after Syria threatened to back the Palestinians Israel called a ceasefire. They accepted UN troops along the Litani River, and began withdrawing troops.

CAMP DAVID AGREEMENT AND PEACE TREATY, 1978–1979

Israel's departure from Lebanon did not stop the civil war which had seen some 50,000 die and allowed Syria to play a major role, but it did satisfy the UN that Israel was keen to revive peace talks with Egypt. The Popular Front for the Liberation of Palestine (PFLP) attacked an Israeli airline crew in London, prompting another Israeli raid on PLO bases in Lebanon. Nonetheless, the peace process got underway again when Sadat and Begin met for talks in Camp David, USA, in September 1978.

Two framework agreements were signed on Sept. 18. The first proposed "full autonomy" for the West Bank and Gaza Strip Palestinians, and specified: i) a "self-governing authority" with powers defined by Israel, Egypt and Jordan, to replace the existing Israeli administration in the areas; ii) a five-year transitional period marked by the staged withdrawal or redeployment of Israeli troops; and iii) negotiations in the third year of this period between Israel, Jordan, Egypt and the Palestinian-elected representatives on the "final status of the West Bank and Gaza". Sadat said Egypt was prepared to assume "the Arab role" if Jordan and the Palestinians refused to participate directly (in the event they did refuse).

The second agreement committed Israel and Egypt to signing a peace treaty within three months, and proposed similar treaties in time between Israel and each of her other neighbours, Jordan, Syria and Lebanon. Two important issues, however, remained unresolved: i) the future of Jewish settlements in the territories, and ii) the status of east Jerusalem (the Israeli government stood by its statement of June 1967 which decreed "Jerusalem is one city indivisible, the capital of Israel").

Because of these stumbling blocks the target date for the treaty was missed, but even so Sadat and Begin were jointly awarded the 1978 Nobel Peace Prize for their efforts. After the personal mediation of President Carter the two sides signed a peace treaty on March 26, 1979, in Washington. Both the Egyptian and Israeli parliaments gave the treaty their overwhelming approval. Instruments of ratification were exchanged at the US surveillance post at Um-Khashiba in Sinai on April 25, thus ending the 31-year-old state of war between Egypt and Israel.

The terms of their new treaty included: i) Israeli military and civilian withdrawal from the whole Sinai peninsula over three years; ii) installation of UN forces in key border areas; iii) restoration of normal diplomatic relations between the countries; iv) guaranteed rights of passage for Israeli shipping and cargo in the Suez Canal; v) the recognition of the Straits of Tiran and Gulf of Aqaba as international waterways; vi) Egyptian agreement to sell Israel oil from her Sinai oilfields; and vii) negotiations towards granting "full autonomy" to the Palestinians of the West Bank and Gaza.

The US government promised both parties that it would "take such action as it may deem helpful to achieve compliance with the treaty" if it were violated, including "the establishment of an acceptable multinational force". However, in a separate "memorandum of understanding" signed with Israel alone, the USA seemed to give a stronger military commitment to Israel. Sadat saw this as a preamble to "an eventual alliance between the US and Israel against Egypt" and rejected it.

PLO REACTION TO "AUTONOMY" PROPOSALS, 1978–1981

Palestinian autonomy was enshrined in the peace treaty, but what it meant in reality was uncertain. Most mayors in the West Bank supported the PLO, and refused to talk with Israel until the latter recognized the organization (on Sept. 1, 1977 the *Knesset* had voted 92 to 4 against negotiations with the PLO).

A wave of bomb attacks in late 1977 and early 1978 against Israeli buses led to mass arrests and administrative detention of alleged *Fatah* and other PLO cells on the West Bank. This coincided with the limited Israeli invasion of south Lebanon in March to flush out guerrilla cells. An estimated 1,000 civilians died in the fighting, along with more than 250 PLO troops. During the same period the PLO admitted responsibility for killing five West Bank Palestinian "collaborators with Israel". Eight died in Jerusalem bomb attacks in June, 1978.

On Oct. 1, 1978, 19 of the 29 West Bank municipalities called for an independent Palestine ruled by the PLO. Israel's hopes for a non-PLO local Palestinian leadership rested with the "village league" movement founded by former Jordanian Minister Mustafa Dudein of Hebron in 1978. These leagues co-operated with the Civil Administration, despite Israel's policy of financially backing Jewish settlements in the territories. By 1983 there were seven leagues claiming 40,000 members, but their power and indeed popularity was limited.

An Arab summit in Baghdad rejected the Camp David agreement on Nov. 8, 1978, and promised aid totalling $3.5 billion to the PLO. Sadat needed Jordan's participation in the talks to make them meaningful, but on March 17, 1979, King Hussein sided with Arafat to form a Joint Committee, whereby funds were given to officials who stayed loyal to Jordan. Hussein agreed to open a PLO political office in Amman. Jordan no longer claimed to "speak for" the Palestinians, having signed the 1974 Rabat agreement. Radical PLO groups and affiliates formed a rival National Guidance Committee in an attempt to stop West Bankers leaving for Jordan.

Renewed PLO raids from Lebanon hardened Begin's position. In July 1979 the Israeli Cabinet voted for "pre-emptive" strikes against PLO bases, rather than mere retaliatory raids. As the military and civilian death tolls mounted with each Israeli raid, the PLO and its leftist Lebanese allies began withdrawing from south Lebanon, leaving it in the hands of Maj. Saad Haddad's anti-PLO Christian forces. They closed down their headquarters in Tyre. On Oct. 4 they announced a ceasefire and an end to raids into Israel. Eight months later they closed their Sidon bases. Begin had succeeded in securing "legitimate self-defence", but at the cost of embarrassing his US ally and antagonizing the UN whose UNIFIL forces were being bypassed.

In 1980 the Lebanon war intensified: Israeli raids continued, authorized by Defence Minister Ezer Weizman; Syrian troops moved into the Bekaa Valley, and some clashed with Israeli troops and their Christian allies; Palestinians now found their former Lebanese Shia allies turn against them. A raid on April 7 by five Palestinian guerrillas of the pro-Iraqi Arab Liberation Front on the Misgav Am kibbutz in Israel gave Begin a pretext for intensified raids on camps in Lebanon. The UN General Assembly condemned Israel for her "aggression" in Lebanon and "terrorist and repressive measures" in the territories.

EGYPTIAN OSTRACIZATION, ISRAELI WITHDRAWAL, 1979–81

On March 31, 1979, all Arab League states except for Sudan and Oman voted to expel Egypt from the League and other joint Arab bodies, to withdraw their ambassadors and to impose an oil embargo. Their decision was echoed by OPEC, the Islamic Conference Organization, the Non-Aligned Movement and the Organization of African Unity. Within Egypt resentment against the treaty grew, exacerbated by economic troubles brought on by the Arab boycott, and by a revival of Islamic fundamentalism inspired by the Iranian revolution. Sadat was assassinated by disaffected army officers on Oct. 6, 1981. However, his successor as President, Hosni Mubarak, reaffirmed Egypt's commitment to the treaty with Israel.

The treaty had also caused splits in Israel. Frustrated at his government's inflexibility on Palestinian autonomy, Dayan resigned as Foreign Minister on Oct. 21, 1979. He was succeeded by Itzhak Shamir, one of the few ministers who had initially rejected the Camp David accords for conceding too much. That same month a new party, *Tehiya* (Rebirth), was founded to reaffirm the "Greater Israel" philosophy many hawks felt Begin had abandoned.

Nonetheless, Israeli withdrawal from the Sinai proceeded smoothly: on Jan. 26, 1980, Egypt and Israel opened their borders; on Feb. 26, 1980 they exchanged ambassadors. There was less success in the autonomy talks. Despite US peace initiatives, these remained log-jammed by Palestinian refusal to participate and Israeli insistence that "full autonomy" could not imply Palestinian sovereignty. *Likud*'s supporters were concerned that there should be no more territorial concessions to Arabs. They were heartened by Israel's destruction of the Osirak nuclear reactor in Iraq on June 8, 1980 which the Cabinet claimed would make atomic weapons for use against them. On July 30, 1980, the *Knesset* consolidated Jerusalem as the "indivisible" capital of Israel. In protest the 13 countries with embassies there all removed them to Tel Aviv. On Dec. 14, 1981, the government effectively annexed the Golan Heights under a decree which extended Israeli law and administration to the former Syrian territory.

Israel thus altered the status of one part of her territory, for which she was lambasted in the UN. The USA joined in the condemnation, but vetoed an attempt to apply sanctions against Israel. Again Israel had embarrassed the USA, because just days before the two had signed a strategic co-operation agreement to counter Soviet threats to the Middle East, and yet had not told her ally of the annexation plan. Although the Heights are comparatively sparsely populated, their annexation suggested the same could be done to other occupied territories. Fears of such incorporation of territories were already heightened by the Israeli cabinet decision of Aug. 24, 1981 to build a canal from the Dead Sea to the Gaza Strip coast. This act was particularly strongly attacked by Egypt, the former custodian of the Strip. On Jan. 6, 1982 it was further announced that 20,000 Jews would settle in the Golan Heights. Local Druze inhabitants went on strike, and Israel blockaded their villages till April.

ELECTIONS AND DIVISIONS IN ISRAEL, 1981–82

The peace talks with Egypt had inspired a new grouping within Israel diametrically opposed to the Land of Israel Movement. Called Peace Now, and uniting the disparate elements of previous "peace fronts", it rejected the Messianism of the settlers and demanded a moratorium on new settlements. It professed "sane Zionism", the belief that security could only come through peace. An end to the state of war with Arab states and lifting of restrictions on Palestinians, it argued, would restore the "normality" dreamt of by the early Zionists. To this end a group of 350 officers and soldiers had protested Begin's encouragement of civilian settlements in 1978. They saw in the subsequent Camp David accords an attempt to annex territory in the five-year transitional stage after the completion of autonomy talks.

When the hardliner Raphael Eitan was appointed Army Chief of Staff, Peace Now protests escalated. In their programme they demanded a repartition of "the land of Israel" and sincere negotiations with Palestinians; but now settlers were regarded as "an arm of the state" and joined "Extended Defence Units". In April 1980 they attacked Palestinian property on the West Bank; next, bombs were planted in the cars of three Palestinian mayors, but the culprits were never punished. When Sharon replaced Weizman as Defence Minister in 1981, the new policy gained official sanction.

Some 5,000 Jews had settled in the Sinai since 1967, and had to leave according to the Camp David accord. To encourage this, the *Likud* government offered financial compensation in January 1982, but hardliners, centred on the town of Yamit, held out till they were forcibly evicted by the Israeli army and the site razed on April 25, 1982. With the withdrawals now complete, Israel went to the polls again and returned a *Likud* government, but many were angry at the mismanagement of the economy—financial liberalization actually boosted inflation, and Finance Minister Hurwitz resigned. Peace activists said resources were diverted to settlements at the expense of Israel proper. With the southern border secure, the Israeli military turned its attention to the north, and the threat posed by a regrouping of PLO cells in southern Lebanon.

IN THE WAKE OF "PEACE FOR GALILEE"

THE LEBANON WAR, SABRA AND CHATILA MASSACRE, 1982

It had long been Israel's proud boast that every war she had fought enjoyed the full backing of her population, was prompted by the enemy and avoided large-scale civilian casualties. After June 1982 she found it harder to make such claims. The attempted assassination by the Abu Nidal group on June 3 of Shlomo Argov, Israeli ambassador to Britain, gave Israel a pretext for invading Lebanon, to her north, on June 6. This was less than two months after the last Israeli troops had withdrawn from the Sinai, and peace was guaranteed for Israel's southern border. The 6,000-strong UNIFIL forces in south Lebanon were powerless to stop Israel's "Peace for Galilee" campaign. Within a month the Israeli Defence Forces had reached the Lebanese capital, Beirut, where an estimated 5,000 PLO fighters were stationed. Hardliners within the Israeli *Knesset*, led by Defence Minister Ariel Sharon, had determined not just to remove the PLO presence south of the Litani River, but to destroy the PLO in all of Lebanon. Allied with Lebanese Phalangist (right-wing Christian) forces, Israeli artillery and aircraft pounded PLO positions and headquarters in Moslem West Beirut throughout August. As PLO fighters were ensconced in civilian areas of the city, many civilians died in the attack.

On Aug. 19, Philip Habib, President Reagan's special envoy in the Middle East, forged an agreement with Israel and Arab states to evacuate all PLO units and Syrian troops of the "Arab Deterrent Force" from Beirut by early September. This was largely achieved, and Israeli troops also withdrew. On Sept. 14, however, Lebanon's president-elect Bashir Gemayel was assassinated. Israeli troops returned and encircled two Palestinian refugee camps outside Beirut, Sabra and Chatila, believing they contained PLO fighters who had avoided evacuation. On Sept. 16–18, Phalangists, seething at Gemayel's death, entered the camps and killed an estimated 700 inhabitants, including women and young children.

At first Israel denied collusion, but following widespread Peace Now demonstrations in the country against the massacre, the Kahan judicial inquiry concluded in February 1983 that various Israeli political and military leaders were responsible for allowing the Phalangists into the camps. As a result of the inquiry, Sharon resigned as Defence Minister; but Begin said Israeli troops would only leave southern Lebanon if there was an overall peace agreement and a stable government in Beirut, and if all 22,000 Syrian troops in the Bekaa Valley left too.

On Dec. 28, 1982, talks between Lebanese and Israeli officials began under US auspices. An agreement was signed on May 17, 1983, agreeing to: i) Israeli withdrawal; ii) an end to the state of war existing between the two countries; and iii) the creation of a "security region" in the south to prevent reinfiltration of the PLO. After months of deterioration, with Israeli units digging in south of the Awali River and Syrians mobilizing in the Bekaa valley and sponsoring Druze attacks on Christians, Lebanon abrogated the treaty on March 5, 1984; Israel decided on unilateral withdrawal in January, 1985. By June 6, 1986, the last troops had departed, but they left behind a six-mile security zone patrolled by their (mainly Christian) proxy militia, the "South Lebanon Army". Cross-border raids by both Israel and returning Palestinian guerrillas continued.

The Lebanese war had a profound effect on both Israelis and Palestinians. The former succeeded militarily in defeating the PLO, but at the ultimate cost of some 650 troops killed. Israel suffered unprecedented national division, including among army conscripts, over the conduct of the war. The Sabra and Chatila incident also angered many supporters of Israel among both foreign governments and Diaspora Jewish communities. On Sept. 25, an estimated 350,000 Israelis protested in the streets of Tel Aviv, the largest demonstration seen in the land.

For their part 12,000 PLO fighters had been forced to leave Beirut and go to neighbouring Arab states. This left behind 237,000 Palestinians registered as refugees with UNWRA, 100,000 with Lebanese, Syrian or Jordanian papers, and 60,000 without papers. An estimated 175,000 displaced refugees required emergency relief. Rumours abounded that the Lebanese government wanted to reduce total Palestinian numbers in the country to 50,000. Israel had captured some 6,000 fighters and placed them in special internment camps. The PLO's political and welfare infrastructure was destroyed and their headquarters

moved from Beirut to Damascus, and later Tunis. Many in the PLO felt
bitter at the Arab League states for not backing up their conference rhetoric
with supportive action in the war.

LIKUD POLICY ON THE WEST BANK, 1981–1984

The war had galvanized Peace Now, but when it ended their attentions
returned to the West Bank. They were joined by new groups, including the
religious *Netivot Shalom* (Paths to Peace) which accepted Israel's ultimate
right to "Greater Israel" but called for territorial compromise if that would
bring peace. Support also grew for extremist groups, like *Kach*, founded
by US-born Rabbi Kahane in 1977, which demanded the expulsion of all
Palestinians from the West Bank.

Since 1967 till the end of 1982, some 109 new settlements were established or
planned, bringing the Jewish population of the territories to 30,000 (compared
with 3,000 when *Likud* came to power). Despite the small numbers of settlers
vis-à-vis both the Jews of Israel and the Palestinians of the territories, their
presence proved highly provocative. In a test case in November 1979 the
Israeli Supreme Court had ruled that seizure of private Arab land for civilian
settlement (as opposed to military) was illegal. The *Likud* government upheld
the ruling, but subsequently sought to bypass it by various means.

On April 10, 1983, they announced a plan to build a further 57 settlements
by 1987, including a number at existing military outposts, and to increase the
settler population to 100,000 by the end of 1985. Labour condemned this as a
"historical mistake", especially the notion of settling near heavily populated
Arab towns like Nablus and Hebron. During the first five months of 1983,
and particularly during President Carter's visit in March, demonstrations and
stone-throwing escalated on the West Bank and Gaza, with students playing
a large role. Jewish settlers retaliated with bomb attacks of their own; 45
Kach members were arrested while trying to take over the Temple Mount in
March; in February four Israeli soldiers were convicted for mistreating Arabs
in 1982.

In July the Mayor of Hebron, Mostafa Natshe, was dismissed after a
Jewish seminary student was killed in the town. Defence Minister Moshe
Arens confirmed plans to "rebuild" the Jewish Quarter in Hebron, but the
government condemned a "revenge" attack by extremists which killed three
Moslem religious students. At the end of the year the *Haaretz* newspaper
ran an opinion poll showing that the proportion of Israelis who opposed

new settlements had grown from about a third of those questioned to almost half.

Nonetheless, by 1984 an estimated 30–40 per cent of land in the territories had been acquired by the Israeli state or by Jewish settlers. About half the Palestinian workforce was employed in Israel, but faced strictures on the formation of independent unions in the West Bank and were not represented by *Histadrut*.

Between January and May, 1984, PLO factions launched four major attacks in Israel, during which many were wounded and seven died. In one incident, Israeli police summarily killed a guerrilla captured after an attempted bus hijack. This prompted official condemnation and criminal proceedings against the police involved.

Israel went to the polls in July 1984 and, after an inconclusive result, *Likud* had to share power with the Labour Alignment. Settlement activity slowed down, and the new Labour Premier Shimon Peres called for talks with Jordan over possible territorial changes. The growing economic crisis overshadowed all other issues, however, and frustrated PLO forces resorted to more acts of violence.

DIPLOMATIC INITIATIVES, VENICE, FEZ AND REAGAN PLANS, 1980–82

While the non-aligned nations were condemning Israel and Egypt for the Camp David accords in Havana in January 1980, the European Community (EC) heads of government issued the "Venice Declaration". This called for mutual recognition of the right to existence and security of all peoples in the Middle East, including Israelis and Palestinians. While praising Israel's departure from the Sinai, it demanded her withdrawal from all areas taken in the 1967 war. Most significantly, breaking with previous pronouncements and with the current US position, it demanded a role for the PLO in future talks. Former Israeli Foreign Minister Abba Eban wrote that now Europe "could not be taken seriously as a disinterested conciliator" in the light of this new stance, which gave no "incentive for moderate Palestinians".

The USA continued its search for peace, but found few willing partners at first. Israel had tried to lessen her military dependence on the USA by developing her own fighter plane, the ill-fated Lavi from March 1980, and exporting arms to countries of her choice. After troubles in Egypt and the toppling of the Shah in Iran, Saudi Arabia, blessed with oil wealth and ruled by traditionalists, became the USA's main non-Israeli ally in the Middle East. On Aug. 8, 1981, Crown Prince (later King) Fahd revealed his own peace plan, which called for a Palestinian state on the West Bank with east Jerusalem as its capital. It broke new ground in tacitly recognizing Israel's right to live in peace. This was denied on Jan. 4, 1982, after the Arab League split over the plan. A planned League summit in Fez had to be aborted on Nov. 25, 1981. Meanwhile Jordan reaffirmed the PLO as sole representatives of the Palestinian people. In a move fiercely opposed by Israel and her US supporters, the US Senate approved a $8.5 billion arms deal with Saudi Arabia on Oct. 28, 1981.

On Sept. 1, 1982, after Israel had invaded Lebanon, US President Reagan revealed his own plan which was similar to the Fahd plan but stopped short of recognizing the PLO. Using Camp David as its "foundation", the plan called for all Arab states to "recognize the reality of Israel, and its right to exist in peace behind secure and defensible borders"; but it also demanded an Israeli freeze on new settlements, withdrawal from the West Bank and Gaza Strip, and after a five-year transitional period, self-government (though not independent statehood) for the Palestinians of the territories "in association with Jordan". The USA further promised to "guarantee Israel's security".

On Sept. 2 the Israeli Cabinet unanimously rejected the plan as a deviation from Camp David, and three days later announced a further $18.5 million towards three new settlements. Jordan and Egypt, however, thought the plan had "positive aspects". Within the PLO, Damascus-based factions wholly rejected it, but Farouk Kaddoumi, the PLO "Foreign Minister", saw some merit in it. A new Fez summit of the Arab League on Sept. 6–9 resuscitated the Saudi plan, reiterating the demand for Israeli withdrawal from the occupied territories. It did, however, alter the Saudi plan in respect of: i) overtly recognizing the "guiding role" of the PLO; ii) giving the duty of peace-keeping in the territories to UN and not Arab forces; and iii) toning down the earlier implicit recognition of Israel. Arab states still refused to negotiate with Israel directly, and insisted on Jerusalem as capital of a future Palestinian state (the Fez plan remains to this day the League's official stance on Israel). On Sept. 10 Israel rejected the plan's call for a mini-state, but US Secretary of State George Schultz said it contained the seeds of a "possible breakthrough".

On Oct. 22, 1982, Reagan met a League delegation to evaluate the two plans. King Hussein had begun to explore the concept of a Palestinian-Jordanian federation with Arafat and met Soviet leader Andropov in early December. On Dec. 21 he visited Washington to discuss Jordan's pivotal role in Palestinian "autonomy" talks. However, the King insisted he could not take part without the full backing of the PLO and the League. During 1983 and 1984 the political horizons of Arafat and Hussein grew closer, culminating in their agreement of 1985, but this moderate approach incensed rebels within the PLO who wished to overthrow Arafat.

DISSENSION IN THE PLO AFTER THE LEBANESE WAR, 1982–1984

The PLO's departure from Beirut in August, 1982, left Syria in a strong position in Lebanon. Damascus felt threatened by Arafat's attempted rapprochement with Jordan, and feared being sidestepped in future peace talks. By 1982 the PLO had representatives in more than 70 countries; Arafat gained further credibility after his audience with the Pope in September. But he was hamstrung in negotiations with Jordan by the need to obtain consensus within the PLO on major issues. Arafat frustrated the "rejectionists" by securing *Fatah*'s dominance of the PLO at the PNC session in Algiers in February, 1983, but in May deadlock gave way to open rebellion. Five senior *Fatah* officers led a mutiny in the guerrilla camps of the Bekaa Valley, accusing Arafat of corruption and lack of commitment to the armed struggle. PFLP and DFLP commanders remained neutral in the conflict but did call for democratic reform within the PLO structure. On June 24 Syria expelled Arafat. Two days later the Grand *Mufti* of Jerusalem issued a religious edict condemning the rebels and calling for the assassination of Syrian President Assad. In July Syrian- and Libyan-backed Palestinian factions, notably the PFLP-GC and the Palestine Liberation Army, joined forces with the *Fatah* rebels and drove Arafat's men out of the Bekaa Valley. The *Fatah* loyalists retreated to Tripoli. Mediation by the USSR and Saudi Arabia failed, and in December Arafat and his 4,000 fighters had to be evacuated in the face of Syrian armed might.

By this stage the PLO had split into three groups: *Fatah* loyalists; an anti-Arafat Damascus-based National Alliance (*Fatah* rebels, PFLC-GC, and *Saiqa*); and a centrist grouping, the Democratic Alliance (PFLP, DFLP, Palestine Communist Party and Palestine Liberation Front). Now a majority of Arab leaders came to Arafat's side, galvanized by a mutual fear of Syria's burgeoning regional strength.

Arab states were impressed by Arafat's ability to secure the release from Israeli prisons of 4,700 PLO detainees in exchange for six captured Israelis held in Tripoli, in December 1983. Within mainstream *Fatah*, some officials had begun talking to Israeli opposition figures in January, 1983. At the February PNC session, Dr Issam Sartawi, chief adviser to the PLO executive committee, resigned after being prevented from making a speech demanding recognition of Israel. On April 10 he was shot dead, allegedly by the Abu Nidal group. Meanwhile the PLO continued to advance towards international respectability. On Aug. 30 a UN Conference on Palestine held in Geneva awarded the PLO the diplomatic status of a sovereign state, and adopted a Programme of Action to create a Palestinian state. Arafat talked with Egyptian President Mubarak on Dec. 22, 1983, and suggested resuming ties though refused to accept the Camp David accords. Attacks against civilians continued however. On Dec. 6 *Fatah* claimed responsibility for a Jerusalem bus bombing which killed five; such actions strengthened the case of Israelis who rejected talks with the PLO.

The two anti-Arafat Alliances met in June 1984 to patch up differences, but progress was slow. They both boycotted the 17th PNC session in November, where the body voted to study Hussein's "territory for peace" plan based on UN Resolution 242. Arafat and Hussein reached agreement on Feb. 11, 1985 to aim at a peace based on a confederation of Jordan and an independent Palestinian state on the West Bank. *Fatah* subsequently denied that it had accepted UN 242, but the fact remains that Arafat was taking a more conciliatory approach, arguably encouraged by the new premiership of Shimon Peres after the 1984 Israeli elections.

COALITION GOVERNMENT IN ISRAEL, 1984–86

On Aug. 28, 1983, Menachem Begin had announced his intention to resign as Israeli Prime Minister; he was succeeded by former Foreign Minister, Itzhak Shamir, on Oct. 10. Begin's departure marked the culmination of a year of troubles for Israel. Major strikes by industrial workers and doctors broke out in 1982 and worsened in 1983. Prominent cabinet ministers resigned on corruption charges. The number of Israelis living below the poverty line had doubled between 1979 and 1981. The poorer, mainly Sephardic, voters felt disillusioned with the *Likud* government as inflation hit their savings. *Likud* was shocked when Labour's nomination for President, Chaim Herzog, was elected by the *Knesset* on March 22, 1983. Rocketing inflation led to two devaluations of the Israeli shekel, in August and October, 1983. In September Shamir held talks with Labour leaders Peres and Rabin to consider a government of national unity, but the latter withdrew over Shamir's policy of continuing West Bank and Gaza settlements.

The government was defeated on a motion opposing their plan to rebuild the Jewish Quarter in Hebron on Feb. 1, 1984. On March 22 the opposition carried a bill calling for new elections. On the eve of the July 22 poll, the following issues divided Israel: i) Lebanon, with the left criticizing *Likud* for putting military conscripts in a compromising position, and for allowing excessive civilian casualties; and with the right critical of the failure to flush out the PLO presence; ii) the 400 per cent rate of inflation, partly fuelled by the Lebanese campaign (*Likud* was condemned for "financial mismanagement"); iii) West Bank settlements and the treatment of Palestinians; iv) the growing gulf between secular Zionists and orthodox Jews, each side claiming to represent the "authentic Israel"; and v) Israel's loss of allies.

In addition, both major groupings were harmed by in-fighting, with Ariel Sharon challenging Shamir's leadership of *Likud*, and the Alignment split between the majority Labour party and the smaller leftist *Mapam*. The Alignment called for a freeze on new settlements and negotiations with Jordan, on a "land for peace" basis, but *Likud* rejected any "territorial compromise". Within the Alignment, Labour promised not to dismantle existing settlements, nor to talk to the PLO, but by so doing they lost the traditional backing of Israel's Arab voters.

In the election voters deserted the two major groupings for the smaller parties and the result was inconclusive. Labour won more votes and seats (44 versus 41) than *Likud*, but failed to muster enough backing from other parties to form a government. Many of these parties won seats in the *Knesset* for the first time, including *Kach* which wanted the forcible expulsion of Palestinians; the Progressive List for Peace (PLP), a joint Arab–Jewish list which called for a Palestinian state in the territories; and *Yahad*, led by former *Likud* Defence Minister Ezer Weizman, which favoured opening talks with the PLO.

After much bargaining, the Alignment and *Likud* agreed on a national coalition government. Peres would be Prime Minister and Shamir Foreign Minister for the first 25 months of a four-year term, with the roles reversed for the remaining 25. In October the new government launched economic austerity measures, which became their first priority. They also announced a package of measures to improve the "quality of life" of West Bank and Gaza Palestinians. These included the opening of an Arab-run bank, licensing of new factories, easing of cash controls and reduction in censorship of Arab magazines. In May 1985 they set up a 10-minister inner cabinet to deal with defence, foreign affairs and the settlements. They also promised to curb Jewish extremist attacks on Palestinians. On April 18, 20 members of the "Jewish Underground" were tried and three sentenced for attacks on Palestinians during 1980–84. On July 31 the *Knesset* banned parties which incited racism.

Nonetheless, attacks from both sides in the territories continued unabated. Economic restraints hindered the development of new settlements, but as before, the houses of convicted Palestinians were often demolished, and many were detained without trial for indefinite periods. On Jan. 10, 1985, the government announced plans for six new settlements by October. In March Bir Zeit University was closed for two months after pro-PLO demonstrations. On Aug. 4 a new ruling allowed for deportation of "persons who constitute a security risk"; at the same time police started investigating alleged fraudulent purchases of Arab land after complaints from 200 landowners. In 1985 the West Bank experienced on average three violent incidents a day, and by March 1986 there was an average of 20 bombings a month. Sixty-two per cent of such incidents were deemed "spontaneous and unlinked to any terrorist organisation", according to former West Bank governor, Binyamin Ben-Eliezer.

Officially, though, the coalition government pursued the Camp David autonomy talks, and sought direct negotiations with Jordan. Relations with Egypt had deteriorated after the recall of the Egyptian ambassador following Sabra and Chatila in 1982, but began improving with talks in late 1984 and early 1985. President Mubarak visited several European states and the USA over the same period. Israel received $2.6 billion in military aid from the USA, and also increased contacts with France, the UK, West Germany and China.

US Secretary of State Schultz proposed in May 1985 that PNC members should participate in a joint negotiating team with Jordan, but Israel rejected this as they saw the PNC as an extension of the PLO. Arafat suggested he would accept UN 242 if the USA accepted Palestinian "self-determination". Hussein proposed a joint Jordanian–PLO team holding an international conference with the USA, leading to direct talks with Israel. In June Peres proposed his own five-stage timetable leading to a conference, and in July the PLO submitted a list of 22 candidates of the PNC to Jordan as possible negotiating partners. These were whittled down to seven and handed to Israel. The Cabinet rejected them, though Peres was quoted as saying two—Hanna Seniora, an editor, and Faez Rahme, a Gaza businessman—were acceptable. Israel still favoured direct talks with Jordan.

An Arab League summit on Aug. 7–9 backed the PLO–Jordan accord, but a spate of terrorist attacks and the Israeli bombing of PLO headquarters in Tunis in October (see below) stymied the peace process. On Oct. 17 Peres announced his willingness for "territorial compromises" and peace with Jordan. Hussein called him a "man of vision", but later Jordan and the PLO rejected his call, and Peres was criticized in his Cabinet for breaking with the Camp David accord.

The spectre of international terrorism returned with attacks on Rome and Vienna airports in late December 1985, allegedly backed by Libya. The US Administration imposed sanctions on Libya and the Israeli Air Force intercepted a Libyan executive jet on Feb. 4, 1986, in the hope of capturing radical PLO leaders. Though condemning Israel's action, the USA itself clashed with Libya in following months.

Meanwhile Peres maintained his efforts for diplomatic progress. On June 22–23, 1986, Peres met King Hassan of Morocco and revealed that they had discussed the 1982 Fez plan. The King later said talks had ended when Peres repeated his refusal to recognize the PLO or withdraw from the territories. In September Peres opened talks with Soviet diplomats. He also met Mubarak in Egypt where they jointly declared 1987 as a "year of negotiations for peace". Peres's initiative for an international conference was halted by his surrender of the premiership to Shamir on Oct. 20, as specified in the coalition agreement. In a speech to the *Knesset*, Shamir restored a commitment to "Greater Israel", though he also spoke of a need to speak to Palestinian residents who renounced the PLO, "the greatest obstacle to peace". By now Israel's economy was at last improving, but political and financial scandals continued, notably the resignation in June of Avraham Shalom, head of Israeli internal security. He was accused of blocking the investigation into the police officers responsible for killing the bus hijackers (see above).

THE BRIEF PLO–JORDAN PACT, PLO UNITY, 1985–87

The Feb. 11, 1985 agreement between Arafat and Hussein proposed a joint Palestinian–Jordanian delegation at peace talks, committed to a Palestine–Jordan confederation and Israeli withdrawal from the territories. Peres welcomed negotiations "without preconditions" with Jordan, but rejected a role for the PLO. On Sept. 25, 1984, Jordan had announced it would restore diplomatic relations with Egypt, an act hailed by Israel as "a victory for the Camp David peace process", and welcomed by *Fatah*. On Feb. 25, 1985 President Mubarak urged US sponsorship of talks and Peres softened his stance. But Arafat's PLO was divided over his rapprochement with moderates—elections at Bir Zeit University returned non-*Fatah* candidates for the first time; PLO executive committee member Fahd Qawasmah was assassinated in Amman on Dec. 29, 1984, for which *Fatah* blamed Syria; a new Palestine National Salvation Front gained support as Damascus accused Arafat of betraying the Palestinian cause;

Moslem fundamentalists on the West Bank and Gaza clashed with the PLO.

Disturbances inside the West Bank were exacerbated by economic crisis in Israel and falling remittances from expatriate Palestinians working in the Gulf. These were mirrored by attacks from outside, notably abortive seaborne raids by *Fatah*, authorized by Arafat's deputy Abu Jihad, in April and May, 1985; rocket attacks on northern Israeli villages and the killing of three Israeli tourists in Cyprus on Sept. 25. Such actions caused Israel to mistrust Arafat's professed new moderation. Throughout 1985 Israel imposed an "iron fist" policy in south Lebanon and carried out several air strikes against PLO bases. On Oct. 1, 1985, Israeli bombers attacked and destroyed the PLO headquarters in Tunis, ostensibly in revenge for the Cyprus incident, and killed up to 70 people. This was followed by a breakaway PLO faction's hijacking of the Italian liner *Achille Lauro*. In response Arafat condemned "terrorism" in a Cairo speech in November, 1985, but said the armed struggle would continue in "occupied territories". Egypt urged the PLO to accept UN resolutions as a step to peace.

Jordan grew impatient with Arafat's inconsistencies and particularly his failure to accept openly UN 242 as a basis for future negotiations. On Feb. 19, 1986, Hussein abrogated his treaty with the PLO, closed all 25 *Fatah* offices in the country and expelled *Fatah* officials. Arafat wanted to preserve the pact with Jordan, but his hopes receded as Jordan began rebuilding ties with Syria. By her actions Jordan inadvertently restored PLO unity, a process that had started in May 1985 when the Lebanese *Amal* militia, assisted by Syria, attacked PLO camps in Bourj-el-Barajneh, Sabra and Chatila. The camps were besieged again in late 1986 and were only relieved when Syrian troops entered in April 1987.

DIPLOMACY AND *INTIFADA*

DIPLOMATIC MANOEUVRING AND INTERNAL UNREST, 1987

Small groups from both Israel and the PLO had held clandestine talks during 1986, though after Aug. 6 a *Knesset* bill banned unauthorized meetings between deputies and the PLO. PLO moderates in turn faced assassination by radicals. On Sept. 4, 1986, Arafat announced in Zimbabwe for the first time that he would support peace talks based on UN 242. On Sept. 8 an opinion poll held on the West Bank revealed that 71.1 per cent expressed loyalty to Arafat, against just 3.4 per cent for King Hussein. Only 17 per cent, however, were prepared to accept a state limited to the West Bank and Gaza.

Violence in the West Bank continued. On Oct. 15, 1986, guerrillas attacked an Israeli Defence Force ceremony in Jerusalem, killing one and wounding 62. *Fatah* claimed responsibility. On Nov. 14 an Israeli religious student was killed in Jerusalem; in December two Palestinian students protesting at Bir Zeit University were shot dead by police, and two stone-throwing boys were killed in Nablus. Two Palestinian newspapers were closed on Aug. 22 for allegedly receiving funds from the PFLP, and on Dec. 28 Akram Haniya became the first Palestinian editor deported from the territories in 14 years.

In early 1987 differing approaches over peace talks widened the divisions in Israel's coalition government. As Foreign Minister, Peres authorized a "peace desk" in his ministry on Jan. 19, and on March 1 called for Israeli participation in a peace conference in a joint communique with Egypt. When a rival bloc of *Likud* Ministers voiced open opposition to this, Peres proposed new elections on May 13. The small *Shinui* party left the government over lack of progress on conference proposals.

Two leading Palestinian moderates were killed—Aziz Shehadah, a lawyer who favoured self-rule, on Dec. 2, 1985; and Zafer al-Masri, who had been appointed Mayor of Nablus to replace the deposed Shaka, on March 2, 1986. Israel appointed three new mayors on Sept. 28 in Ramallah, Hebron and Bira. In early 1987 there were three guerrilla attacks inside Israel, and on April 19 *Fatah* forces crossed the Lebanese border and killed two Israeli soldiers near Kiryat Shemona. In a controversial decision the cabinet had voted to increase university fees for students not eligible for military service, in effect discriminating against Palestinians. Following student protests the proposal was dropped on May 28. A report in January claimed that only 20 per cent of settlements were economically viable.

Israel's relations with traditional allies became increasingly strained in 1987. The UK protested over the use of forged British passports by *Mossad* agents. The US government was upset at apparent official Israeli backing for the actions of Jay Pollard, a US citizen convicted for spying for Israel, and over alleged Israeli customs discrimination against Black and Arab US citizens. In addition, the USA was embarrassed about Israel's role in the Iran–Contra arms deal scandal. Elsewhere Israel fared better: Shamir toured West Africa in mid-June, and five African states restored diplomatic relations broken in 1973; new links were forged with Ireland, Yugoslavia, the USSR, West Germany and South-East Asian countries. Egypt and Israel held their first summit meeting since 1981 on Sept. 11, 1986.

THE 18TH PNC SESSION, SUPPORT FOR CONFERENCE IN ISRAEL

Within the PLO there was intense bargaining to achieve accord on the eve of the 18th PNC session. On March 19–23, 1987 Col. Kadhafi of Libya hosted a conference in Tripoli of all the major anti-Arafat PLO groupings. It demanded formal abrogation by the PLO of the defunct Amman accords, and criticized i) any attempts by Arafat to achieve peace based on UN resolutions, ii) relations with Egypt, and iii) limits on the extent of armed struggle. On April 19 the PLO formally abrogated the accord with Jordan. The next day, PFLP leader Habash announced the end of the Palestine National Salvation Front. Most major PLO groupings, including the Abu Nidal group, turned up for the PNC meeting, the sole boycotters being the *Fatah* rebels, Saiqa, and the PFLP-GC.

At the session, held in Algiers on April 20–25, 1987, the PNC reaffirmed the aim of creating a Palestinian state with Jerusalem as its capital. One DFLP spokesman claimed the state would be limited to the West Bank and Gaza, but officially the PNC rejected any "partial" or bilateral solutions. It nonetheless welcomed an international conference with PLO participation, and stressed the "special and distinctive relationship" between Palestinians and Jordanians. The PNC also endorsed the Fez plan, but rejected negotiations based on UN 242 and 338 including the Reagan and Camp David plans, as well as the "Jordanian option". Salah Khalaf (Abu Iyad) stated that Palestinian delegates to a conference need not be PLO members themselves. The PNC called for better relations with Syria, though radicals won a motion insisting on a complete breach with Egypt as long as it kept to the Camp David accords. Egypt accordingly closed the PLO office in Cairo. In apparent contravention of the resolution, Arafat chaired a special committee in May to improve relations with Egypt, and the PLO Cairo office was reopened on Nov. 29. Explaining the presence of the Abu Nidal group, Abu Iyad said the PLO was "testing" them to see if they would abandon terrorism.

On April 28 Israeli newspapers reported that Peres and Defence Minister Rabin had met King Hussein and agreed terms for an international conference based on UN resolutions. The report was subsequently denied by both sides. On May 4 Arafat responded to calls by Ezer Weizman and declared his willingness to meet Shamir to discuss an Israeli–Palestinian state with dual nationality. Later Peres met the Soviet ambassador to the USA to discuss Soviet participation in a conference, and on May 21 the US ambassador to Israel said Jordan, Egypt and the USA had agreed on a framework for the conference, whereby participants would have to renounce terrorism and abide by UN resolutions. A flurry of diplomatic moves ensued in June and July, involving Israel, Egypt and European states; but by August Prime Minister Shamir was denouncing the conference proposals as "an idea of suicide and surrender".

From Jordan's perspective, the PNC session conveyed ambiguity. On March 27, 1986, the Jordanian House of Representatives had been expanded to officially represent more West Bank Palestinians. Now it appeared that the PLO rejected Jordan's right to administer the territories, but that left Israel with more *de facto* power, as shown by the appointment of mayors. Israel in turn conveyed mixed messages: on Feb. 9, 1987, the first Arab Israeli diplomat took office in the USA; on Feb. 16, police closed down the pro-Palestinian Israeli-run Alternative Information Centre in Jerusalem. Meanwhile the escalation of the Iran–Iraq war had reunited Arab nations opposed to the Ayatollah. Egypt benefited from this, and after an Arab League summit in Amman on Nov. 8–11, nine states (including Iraq and Saudi

Arabia) announced restored relations with Egypt. Simultaneously Egypt drew closer to Israel, with Foreign Minister Meguid visiting Tel-Aviv on July 20 to discuss peace.

The Israeli government, however, had no clear peace policy as Peres backed an international conference while Shamir insisted on bilateral talks. In a bid to break the deadlock, US State Department official Charles Hill toured the region with a new plan for a "mini-conference" of Israel, Egypt and a joint Jordanian–Palestinian delegation. In part this was designed to allay Israeli fears of a Soviet role in a larger conference. Israel cautiously welcomed the proposal but King Hussein rejected it. The USSR softened its stance, saying non-PLO delegates "acceptable to the PLO" should attend talks.

On Sept. 15, 1987 the USA announced it would close the PLO's information bureau in Washington, and on Dec. 16 the House of Representatives voted to close the PLO's office at the UN in New York. It was alleged that pro-terrorist elements were operating from the offices, but the actions resulted in UN condemnation, and a Palestinian boycott of Shultz's visit to Israel in October. On Sept. 7, Arafat met left-wing Israeli deputies, led by Charlie Biton, and reportedly proposed direct talks with Israel. On Sept. 18 two leading *Likud* men, Moshe Amirav and Ehud Olmert, revealed that they had held talks with pro-PLO West Bank academics Faisal Husseini and Sari Nusseibeh. Future talks were curtailed after PLO–Israeli clashes in Lebanon, attacks on Nusseibeh by radical Palestinians and the administrative detention of Husseini.

OUTBREAK OF *INTIFADA*, DECEMBER 1987

While Middle Eastern nations entertained the prospect of a settlement, tensions between Israelis and Palestinians mounted in south Lebanon and in the territories. *Amal* launched fresh attacks on refugee camps near Sidon in Lebanon, and battles spread to Beirut by October. In the south the PLO joined forces with *Hezbollah* fighters and fought against Israeli and South Lebanese Army forces. The Israeli Air Force strafed the Ein al Hilwe camp near Sidon on Sept. 5, 1987 killing an estimated 50 people. On Sept. 15, three Israeli soldiers were killed in a clash with guerrillas near the Israeli border.

Violence in the territory continued to escalate. In February and March 1987 stone-throwing and deportations of Palestinians spread from Gaza to the West Bank and Golan Heights. On April 17 a Jewish settler died when his car was petrol-bombed; Bir Zeit University was shut for four months and 80 Palestinians were arrested in Gaza. In June, settlers from Kiryat Arba raided the Dehaishe refugee camp near Bethlehem. In July the entire Gaza Strip was placed under curfew after the killing of the military police commander. In September the head of the Israeli civil administration in the West Bank, Brig.-Gen. Ephraim Sneh, resigned after conflict with his hardline colleagues. By this stage several Palestinians had died.

Evidence grew of new co-operation between *Fatah* and Islamic fundamentalist groups. In previous years they had fought each other. The pre-eminent group was the Islamic *Jihad*, based in the Gaza Strip. Violence escalated there in early October when seven Palestinians were killed by Israeli police and army in two incidents. Following the earlier pattern, unrest spread to the West Bank, and on Nov. 2 the PLO called for a general strike to mark the anniversary of the Balfour Declaration, to which most Palestinian businesses responded. On Nov. 25 the Israeli Defence Force was embarrassed when a lone Palestinian gunman on a hang-glider flew into northern Israel from Lebanon and killed six Israeli troops.

The actual trigger for what became known as the *intifada* happened on Dec. 8. Four Palestinian labourers died when an Israeli taxi crashed into them near the Jabalaya refugee camp. Camp residents claimed the crash was deliberate, and attacked Israeli patrols who responded with live ammunition. Two died, and another eight were killed by police fire in Nablus by Dec. 14. While troops quelled sympathetic violence in Gaza, unrest continued on the West Bank and spread to Israel itself on Dec. 20 when Arabs in Jaffa, Lod and Nazareth responded to a PLO call for a day of protest against Israeli actions.

By the end of the year, some 900 Palestinians had been arrested. Within Israel the army was criticized for using live ammunition. The army defended its actions, saying soldiers only used gunfire as a last resort when their own lives were in danger. Thereafter officers ordered troops to use batons and rifle-butts to quell violence. Egypt and the USA condemned Israeli actions, but the latter abstained from a UN Security Council resolution on Dec. 22, "deploring the violation of the human rights of the Palestinian people".

IMPOSITION OF THE "IRON FIST" POLICY, 1988

On Jan. 3, 1988, nine Palestinians were served with deportation orders for "incitement and subversive activities". For the first time since 1981 the USA voted with other UN Security Council members in condemning Israeli policy. On Jan. 4 UK Foreign Minister David Mellor visited the West Bank and caused controversy in Israel after he strongly criticized conditions in refugee camps. Violent demonstrations spread after Jan. 5, with gangs of youths (the *shabiba*) erecting barricades of burning tyres in Gaza. From Jan. 11 leaflets appeared, eventually bearing the title "PLO—United National Leadership of the Uprising", and Radio Al-Quds, a pro-PFLP-GC station, began broadcasting from Syria.

By Jan. 12, 35 Palestinians had been killed and 250 wounded. All eight Gaza refugee camps were blockaded by the Israeli military, and trucks of UNWRA and sympathetic Israelis carrying food and medicine into the camps prevented from entering. Arab workers from the territories boycotted work in Israel, some willingly, others after intimidation by *intifada* leaders. Repercussions were being felt in the Israeli economy. On Jan. 15 Border Police (largely Druze units) clashed with Moslem worshippers at the Mosque of Al-Aqsa in Jerusalem and 70 were wounded in beatings and tear-gassing. Soon after police imposed a curfew on certain Arab neighbourhoods in Jerusalem.

The Cabinet on Jan. 17 endorsed an "iron fist" policy to deal with unrest, though Shamir and Defence Minister Rabin appeared to be more enthusiastic about this than Foreign Minister Peres. Rabin stated that "the first priority is to use might, power and beatings" to restore order. Later he backtracked somewhat, warning that soldiers engaging in "deviations . . . would be dealt with". Under emergency powers, Israel restricted access to journalists, and detained a number of Palestinian writers. UN Under Secretary-General Marrack Goulding was prevented from entering a refugee camp. Reports emerged from Israeli hospitals of deaths from beatings, and elsewhere it was reported that collective punishment was being meted out to families of those arrested. A short lull in violence was broken in February, when more teenagers were killed in Nablus and Jerusalem.

Two new trends began emerging: retaliation by Jewish settler groups in the West Bank, and a spreading of unrest away from the camps to the traditionally quieter villages. Now Israeli liberals joined the chorus of disapproval from the UN, USA and EC countries. On Feb. 14 the first Israeli troops were arrested and later sentenced for an incident near Nablus involving the "live burial" of arrested Palestinians. As a result Rabin announced a stricter "code of conduct" for soldiers. A visit by George Shultz to Israel on Feb. 20–21 prompted fierce protests, and on Feb. 23 the first Palestinian collaborator was lynched after he shot at a mob attacking his house near Jenin. The televised systematic beating by soldiers of two youths arrested for stone-throwing caused consternation among many Israelis and prompted the West Bank military commander, Gen. Amram Mitzna, to warn the army not to become a "rabble". By Feb. 25, 83 Palestinians had died in violence, mostly from gunshots; by the end of March it was 120.

On March 10 the European Parliament condemned Israeli actions and expressed "solidarity with the families of the victims and with all Palestinians throughout the region". Undaunted, Israeli authorities banned fuel deliveries to the territories, cut telephone links, closed markets and restricted financial movements. Palestinians responded with a tax boycott, and by March 15 half of the 1,000 Arab policemen in the territories had resigned their commissions, following similar moves by the heads of the "village leagues" and tax officials. On March 20, the first Israeli died in the *intifada*, a soldier shot while on guard duty in Bethlehem.

JORDAN RENOUNCES CLAIM TO WEST BANK

The *intifada* gave a fresh impetus to peace efforts. On Dec. 11, 1987, the UN General Assembly voted that all member states back an international peace conference. On Jan. 24 Arab League foreign ministers voted unanimously to support an "insurrection fund" set up by the PLO. West German Foreign Minister Hans-Dietrich Genscher and Egyptian President Mubarak toured Middle Eastern and European countries respectively in mid-January, 1988, with peace proposals. Mubarak called for a six month truce and freeze on settlements as a precursor to a conference. Rumours abounded that Rabin had sent messages to Arafat requesting a "ceasefire". After pro-PLO demonstrations in Jordan, Cabinet ministers there reopened contacts with the PLO. On Feb. 5, US Assistant Secretary of State Richard Murphy began a shuttle tour of the Middle East in Damascus, where he outlined a new US plan: an international conference leading to six months of autonomy negotiations, Israeli withdrawal from the Judean hills, direct talks on Dec. 1, Palestinian elections in 1989, and three years' grace before a permanent settlement.

Peres welcomed the plan, but Shamir called it "impractical" and accused Peres of selling out. The PLO rejected the plan as it did not mention PLO participation or an intention to create a Palestinian state. Mubarak lamented the US attachment to "the outdated formula of Camp David"; but Jordan gave Shultz some cautious encouragement. Shamir visited the USA in March, reiterating his opposition to any "territory for peace" scheme, to which President Reagan declared: "Those who say 'no' to the plan need not answer to us. They'll need to answer to themselves and their people . . ." Many traditionally pro-Israeli US Senators expressed dismay at Shamir's inflexibility. For the first time the US Jewish community was openly divided.

On Feb. 12, 1988, three Abu Nidal members were sentenced to life imprisonment in Rome for earlier attacks on Rome and Vienna airports. That same day three leading PLO officers were killed in a bomb blast in Cyprus. The PLO blamed *Mossad*. On March 15 another bomb in Cyprus damaged a ferry which the PLO hired to ship 100 Palestinian deportees back to Israel. A group called *Kach International* claimed responsibility. In response, Arafat hinted that the PLO would resume attacks outside Israel.

After a spate of demonstrations and occasional bomb blasts by Jordanian Palestinians in sympathy for the *intifada*, King Hussein announced on July 31, 1988, that Jordan would give up its administration of the West Bank, and allow the Palestinians to "secede" and form their own state. Jordan also ended its West Bank development plan and dissolved the extended House of Representatives. The PLO had rejected both plans as attempts to perpetuate Jordanian sovereignty over the West Bank. On Aug. 2–3 the PNC stated that the PLO would take over responsibilities in the territories. Jordan responded by ending its payment of salaries to 18,000 Palestinian civil servants in the area.

THE PLO RECOGNIZES ISRAEL AND DECLARES A PALESTINIAN STATE

Encouraged by the *intifada* and by the successful hang-glider raid in November 1987, several PLO factions launched attacks from outside against Israel in 1988. The most notable incident was the hijacking of a bus carrying workers to the Dimona nuclear plant in the Negev Desert on March 7 by Palestinians from Egypt. During the resultant clash with soldiers, all three gunmen and three passengers were killed.

The *de facto* deputy leader of the PLO, Khalil al-Wazir (Abu Jihad), was assassinated in Tunis on April 16, 1988; the attack was widely blamed on Israel. Abu Jihad was reportedly planning the "second stage" of the *intifada*, to include attacks on selected Israeli military targets. An estimated crowd of 500,000 attended his funeral in Damascus, including both pro- and anti-Arafat factions. Arafat himself met Syrian President Assad four days later, but the apparent unity between the two former enemies was strained by fierce attacks on *Fatah* camps in Lebanon by Syrian-backed *Fatah* rebels. By July, pro-Arafat forces were driven from the Chatila and Bourj al-Barajneh camps. Throughout the year Israeli forces attacked Palestinian camps outside Sidon, and clashed with *Hezbollah*.

Nonetheless, mainstream PLO officials began exploring compromises to reach peace with Israel. They were encouraged by growing opposition within Israel to the iron fist policy, as evidenced by the formation of a new Centre Party on Feb. 2 willing to talk with them if they would recognize Israel; and by the successes of the *Yesh Gvul* ("There is a Limit") movement, which encouraged a small yet vociferous minority of soldiers to refuse to serve in the territories.

Israel celebrated its 40th anniversary of independence on April 21, 1988 and signed a five-year memorandum of understanding with the USA which provided for regular consultations between leaders and joint military exercises. Throughout 1988 Israel sought to improve ties with Soviet bloc countries, China and Japan, but the *intifada* hindered progress.

At the Algiers Arab League summit in June, Jordan pledged its support for the PLO. Bassam Abu Sharif, a close adviser to Arafat, then revealed a conciliatory plan calling for a "two-state solution", after PLO–Israeli negotiations under UN auspices. The PLO, he added, was willing to run against other Palestinian candidates nominated by Israel or the USA in a referendum to be held in the territories. After the summit, which had reaffirmed the 1982 Fez peace plan, reports emerged that Saudi Arabia and various Gulf states had pledged $118 million towards sustaining the *intifada*. By July rumours emerged that Israeli and PLO officials had met in Romania to discuss how to end the *intifada* and reach a settlement, although Shamir denied this.

The real victory for PLO moderates, however, took place at the 19th session of the PNC. In the months leading up to it, the PLO leadership prepared the ground for a historic compromise. In August members of the Palestine Central Council (advisers to the PLO) toured Jordan and Egypt to work out how to fill the gap left by Jordan's renunciation of the West Bank. Arafat met UN Secretary-General Perez de Cuellar to seek a UN role in the solution, and on Sept. 13 he addressed the socialist group of the European Parliament and called for Israeli recognition of a Palestinian state and immediate talks based on UN resolutions. Meanwhile he would prepare a provisional government. On Oct. 10, the PLO leadership met in Tunis and planned their statement for the next PNC meeting. Then Arafat, Mubarak and Hussein met in Jordan to co-ordinate policy between the three for an international conference.

On Nov. 12–15, 1988, the 19th PNC session met in Algiers. All PLO factions, apart from the PFLP-GC, *Saiqa* and *Fatah* rebels, were present. At the end of the session the PNC proclaimed a Palestinian state with Jerusalem as its capital, in accordance with UN Resolution 181 (1947) which had advocated the partition of Palestine. The PNC declared its intention to set up a provisional government, and added a "political statement" calling for an international conference with all five UN Security Council member states and the PLO present, on the basis of UN Resolutions 242 and 338. In the interim the occupied territories "should be placed under UN supervision . . . to protect our people and create a suitable atmosphere (for a conference)". Finally, the PNC voted to reject terrorism in all its forms, including "institutionalized terrorism", and repeated the earlier commitment restricting violence to Israel and the occupied territories. PFLP leader Georges Habash voted against the statement, but said that he would accept a majority vote.

INTERNATIONAL REACTIONS TO THE PLO DECLARATION

Immediately all Arab states (except for Syria) recognized the Palestinian state, as did countries from the Non-aligned Movement and China. The USSR recognized the proclamation, but not the state itself. Israel denounced the declaration and began campaigning against it. The USA said the PLO statements were "an advance" but still "too vague". They criticized its failure to overtly recognize Israel and condemn terrorism unequivocally, preconditions of US acceptance of a PLO role at a conference. On Nov. 26 the US State Department refused Arafat an entry visa to address the UN General Assembly in New York, on the grounds that he "condoned and lent support to" acts of terrorism. The General Assembly met instead in Geneva on Dec. 13–15. Meanwhile Arafat toured various Arab states to assess their support for his initiative, and on Dec. 6 met an American–Jewish delegation in Sweden. Afterwards the delegation said they were sure that the PLO now recognized Israel and had abandoned terrorism, and thus felt that talks between the USA and the PLO should proceed.

At the Geneva UN session, Arafat elaborated on his PNC statement, calling for a UN peacekeeping force to oversee Israeli withdrawal from the territories. This time the USA responded more favourably, and after a further statement from Arafat explicitly recognizing Israel and "totally renouncing" terrorism, George Shultz authorized Robert Pelletreau, US ambassador to Tunisia, to open negotiations with PLO officials. "Practical and constructive" talks took place between the USA and the PLO for the first time in Tunis on Dec. 16. Israel, however, voiced official regret at the US decision. The UN General Assembly adopted a resolution calling for an international conference with PLO representation.

The diplomatic initiative had little effect on the *intifada*, however. As it entered its second year on Dec. 9, 1988, renewed strikes and demonstrations broke out. According to the Palestine Human Rights Information Centre, 393 Palestinians had died in the unrest, 298 from army fire, and 95 through beatings and tear-gassing. Among the most noteworthy incidents in the period since March were: the accidental shooting of an Israeli girl by a Jewish settler guard when a Jewish hiking party was threatened by Palestinians, April 6; the killing of 14 demonstrators protesting Abu Jihad's assassination, April 16; the reopening of schools in East Jerusalem and on the West Bank, May 22–29; the granting of permission to settlers to open fire if attacked by petrol bombs, June 17; a split between the Islamic *Hamas* resistance and the PLO-led United National Leadership over the former's call for a West Bank strike, Aug. 9; the banning of Palestinian "popular committees" and the deportation of 25 of their leaders, Aug. 17–18; Rabin's announcement of a new "shoot-to-wound" policy, Sept. 27; the murder of two Palestinian "collaborators", Oct. 6; and the shooting of a three-year-old girl after riots in Gaza, Nov. 9.

On Feb. 7, 1989, the US State Department published figures claiming that 366 Palestinians had died and more than 20,000 had been wounded in the *intifada*, compared with 11 Israelis killed and 1,100 wounded. It further alleged that several of the 10,000 imprisoned Palestinians had been tortured, that over 150 houses had been demolished or sealed as punishment and that there were "increasing restraints" on freedom of speech and press in the territories. On Feb. 8 the Israeli Defence Forces condemned the report for lack of balance and its failure to consider the way in which soldiers were "humiliated and challenged" by rioters. Human rights, it said, remained "a basic tenet of Israel's conduct".

ISRAELI ELECTIONS, NOVEMBER 1988

In general elections on Nov. 1, 1988, Israelis were confronted with the need to choose a new government in the light of the *intifada* and the PLO's unprecedented offer of peace. Internationally, Israel was being criticized in many formerly favourable quarters for not welcoming the PLO offer. Even among Diaspora Jewish communities there was dissent.

As before, the election yielded no clear victor, although it returned a stronger *Likud* (40 seats to the Labour Alignment's 39) with a comparatively strong showing for the religious Sephardic *Shas* (six seats). A pre-election opinion poll showed that 54 per cent of Israelis favoured talks with the PLO if they were sincere about peace; but right-wing parties spoke openly of "transferring"

Palestinians from the territories. On the day of the election a petrol bomb was thrown at a bus, killing an Israeli woman and her child. This event, claimed the Labour Alignment afterwards, robbed it of the chance of winning the election on a platform of negotiations. After much acrimonious internal bargaining, the Alignment chose to join the government as a junior partner without control over foreign policy. By so doing the two major groupings jettisoned an alliance with a reinvigorated religious bloc (18 seats in all). Thus they avoided having to make concessions on contentious religious matters; yet in their coalition accord they made no mention of peace proposals, a potentially divisive issue. As Finance Minister, Peres announced a new economic austerity plan on Jan. 1, 1989, but Defence Ministry sources stressed that the Army's operations in the territories would not be affected. On Jan. 17 Rabin lifted curbs on the army's use of firearms in the *intifada*, and called for more collective punishments such as the demolition of houses. More Palestinians were killed in January than in any month since March 1988.

On Jan. 2, 1989 the EC Council of Ministers announced a fresh plan for a Middle East conference. New Israeli Foreign Minister Moshe Arens called it "well intentioned" but reminded the EC countries that they "are not exposed to the mortal dangers that Israel has had to face". On Jan. 13, William Waldegrave, a UK Foreign Minister, met Arafat in Tunisia in the first such contact between the UK and the PLO. Israel condemned the meeting, together with Waldegrave's subsequent statement comparing PLO terror with Shamir's own alleged involvement in the murder of Lord Moyne in 1944.

In a new Soviet initiative, Foreign Minister Eduard Shevardnadze went on a tour of five countries in the region during February 1989. In Syria, he warned Assad that if he did not resume ties with the PLO and consider peace with Israel, Soviet aid would dry up. In Egypt he met Mubarak, Arens and Arafat on Feb. 19–20, and on Feb. 23 he outlined a plan of secure superpower co-operation to achieve peace in the region. Though he identified as central the realization of Palestinian self-determination, he acknowledged Israel's right to security within recognized borders, guaranteed by the UN.

Across the Atlantic, Arens visited Washington on March 13, to be told by US Secretary of State James Baker that Israel should reduce its troop presence in Palestinian towns, free detained Palestinians and reopen schools in the territories. Palestinians in turn should end violent protests and cease raids from Lebanon. (These had recently intensified, leading Israel to question Arafat's vow to end terrorism). In renewed US–PLO talks on March 22, the USA stressed the need to "reduce tension" before agreeing to a conference, while the PLO wanted more immediate US pressure on Israel. Arafat's status was boosted on March 16, when the Islamic Conference recognized the newly declared state of Palestine; and on April 1, when the PLO council voted unanimously to nominate him as President of the state.

THE SHAMIR PLAN 1989

Within Israel a lobby for talks with the PLO was gathering strength. Equally right-wing elements put pressure on Shamir's government to forego talks, and take a tougher line with protesters. On Feb. 26 Arafat gave his first press conference for Israeli journalists, in Cairo, on the occasion of Egypt and Israel signing a final agreement on the disputed Taba strip. Shortly after Abba Eban and Faisal Husseini shared a platform at a peace symposium in Israel. A video of Salah Khalaf (Abu Iyad) was relayed, where he said the PLO sought "co-existence" with Israel. On March 8 former director of Israeli military intelligence, Aharon Yariv, issued a report saying that Palestinian statehood was inevitable. Welcomed by Peres, the report proposed a 15-year transitional period before the state's creation. Another secret intelligence report calling for talks with the PLO was leaked on March 20. In early April US President Bush played host to Mubarak and Shamir. The latter unveiled a plan rooted in Camp David for elections in the territories to help form a non-PLO delegation for negotiations. Initially rejected out of hand by PLO and Arab leaders, Abu Iyad later suggested that PNC candidates stand in UN-supervised polls.

The beginning of the Moslem fast of Ramadan saw new violence in Jerusalem, with Palestinians attacking soldiers and Jews praying at the Western Wall. On April 10 a Palestinian was shot dead in the Old City; an ultra-nationalist Jewish group, the Sicarites, claimed responsibility. On April 13 Israeli Border Police killed four and wounded 15 Palestinians in an incident at Nahalin, south of Bethlehem, drawing protests from the Red Cross and Amnesty International. Another three were killed on April 16, the first anniversary of Abu Jihad's death.

On May 16 the Cabinet approved by 20 votes to six a new 20-point plan. In a key concession, Shamir accepted "free regional and political" Palestinian elections, rather than just a municipal poll. Nonetheless, he ruled out negotiations with the PLO, a freeze on settlements or any exchange of land for peace. In search of support for the plan, Shamir visited Britain while Arens travelled to the USA, but both were rebuffed. James Baker warned that "Israel (must) lay aside once and for all the unrealistic vision of a 'Greater Israel'"; UK Prime Minister Margaret Thatcher reportedly said the plans "did not go far enough". For his part, Shamir reiterated that a PLO state would be "a new

Lebanon . . . and mean the destruction of Israel". He said that until the PLO abandoned its Charter, he would not accept the veracity of Arafat's recent moderate statements. The Arab League summit, with Egypt readmitted, met on May 23 in Morocco and backed the PLO in rejecting the plan. But cracks appeared in the PLO show of unity, as the PFLP's Habash claimed Arafat had no mandate to recognize Israel without a reciprocal recognition by Israel of the PLO.

Within the Israeli Cabinet, Ariel Sharon condemned Shamir for conceding too much. On June 6 Israel imposed a six-day, 24-hour curfew on the Gaza Strip. It ended when Egyptian Foreign Minister Butros-Ghali visited Israel for the first time since the *intifada* started, to learn more about the elections plan. On June 19 an Israeli from Ariel, a West Bank "commuter suburb", was stabbed to death while hiking, prompting settler demonstrations outside Shamir's office. Meanwhile two ministers, Moshe Shahal and Ezer Weizman, called for dialogue with the PLO.

Shamir came under increasing right-wing pressure to modify his plan, and on July 5 he made a firm commitment to reject forever a Palestinian state and exclude East Jerusalem Palestinians from voting in the elections, thus making it virtually impossible for PLO leaders to go along with the initiative. Sixteen hours later news broke of a Gaza Strip Palestinian who forced an Israeli bus to crash, killing 14 passengers. In the wake of national outrage, Peres, Rabin and other Labour politicians who opposed Shamir's concessions to the right postponed a move to leave the government in protest. By July 14 it seemed a compromise was reached, and Labour voted narrowly to stay in the coalition, explaining to their left wing that to leave office would close the door on any chances of peace.

Likewise within the territories there were reports of various splits—between those *Fatah* elements willing to accept parts of a Shamir plan (including a partial withdrawal of Israeli forces from the territories) and those Communists and PFLP followers who rejected the plan entirely; between Moslem forces (Islamic Jihad and *Hamas*) and secular (the United Leadership); between grassroots activists and external PLO leaders. Nonetheless, after 20 months the *intifada* showed little sign of abating. Would a *Likud* government ever negotiate with the PLO; and if they did, would PLO rebels allow Arafat to negotiate with them? After 41 years of the State of Israel, the chances for a resolution to the Palestinian problem have never appeared so distant, nor so close.

PART II:

REPORTAGE
EXPERT BRIEFINGS
REFERENCE SECTION

Welcome to the refugee camp (*Martin Wright*)

Greeting relatives across the border at Rafah, Gaza Strip (*Tordai*)

REPORTAGE

TEL AVIV BY NIGHT

Elfi Pallis

Tel Aviv's sprawling central bus station in the evening rush hour is no place for the faint-hearted, and so it was good to suddenly see Ahmed among the jostling crowds. Although not so much a friend as an acquaintance, I would have recognized him anywhere. The only Arab in an English course I had taken many years ago, he had a round, cherubic face that would remain calm even during the toughest political debate and hid a sharp, largely self-taught mind. We agreed that the coincidence called for a drink, but as there was no later bus to his Galilee village he proposed to invite along a cousin working nearby who could put him up for the night.

On the way to the other man's workplace, Ahmed told me that he had taken his matriculation exam after our course, but was now a building worker. Sensing my surprise, he explained that it was hard to find white collar jobs that were not reserved for "army leavers", a category of people I had often seen mentioned in newspaper ads without ever taking in that it excluded Israel's Arab citizens.

Still, he felt he had been more fortunate than the cousin we were to meet, whose family had fled from a neighbouring village in 1948 and had lived in West Bank refugee camps ever since. His village was now a prosperous kibbutz.

Khalil, Ahmed's cousin, turned out to be working in a small 1930s brick building fronted by a rather grand cast iron gate. A tarnished copper plate showed it to be a factory of "baked goods". It was now 8 pm and getting dark, but the lights in the windows showed that the working day here wasn't over yet. Pushing open the door, I found myself opposite what seemed to be the accounts office, judging by its ledgers and the fact that its occupant was talking into his telephone in rapid Romanian, the mother tongue of most Israeli accountants. Replacing the receiver, he asked what my business was, and when I told him gruffly ordered me to wait outside.

There I found Ahmed talking to his cousin through a small barred window. Looking inside, my face was hit by a gust of scorching air. The poky room on the other side was dominated by a huge cast-iron oven linked to a kind of ferris wheel that periodically turned with a shrill screech, tipping something into the oven. The walls of the room were black with soot, as were the faces of the men mixing dough and stacking trays. They were half-naked and dripping with sweat.

The oven itself, however, looked freshly polished and pristine. Engraved on its smooth top were the name of its makers and the words "Darmstadt, 1934" in ornate gothic letters. Hopelessly unsuited to the Mediterranean climate, it had presumably been imported from Germany in response to an early Nazi law allowing Jews to take out only machinery, not money.

Eventually, the cousins stopped talking and we returned to the front entrance. The door soon opened to reveal Khalil, now cleaned up, talking in Arabic to a plump man who could have passed for Ahmed's twin, had he not been wearing a large, golden Star of David pendant. Once the man had waved him off, Khalil joined us, murmuring as we walked away: "He hates letting us go, even though he used to work the machines himself until the boss made him manager." Did he always work such a long day? "Not always", he said, "but we from the territories finish off the job after the others have gone". The others, it emerged, were Arabs living inside Israel's pre-1967 borders.

"You must find a lot of things changed here, having lived abroad for so long", said Ahmed. "See what an aggressive people we are, we have conquered your factories!"

To illustrate the point, Khalil waved at two faces in the window of another factory and exchanged some banter. "Poor things, they'd like to come along, but they can't. They sleep on the shop floor and the boss locks them in at night to make sure they don't get into trouble." "It's true. Lots of employers do it nowadays, it's cheaper than hiring them a room", added Ahmed, clearly expecting disbelief. In fact, the evening papers had carried a story about two Arab workers burnt when the workshop they were locked into at night had caught fire.

The men proposed that we go to a café in Jaffa, but I fancied the bright lights of Dizengoff Square so we set out there. Grey and bureaucratic during the day, the city centre is a riot of colour at night. Cafés suddenly light up, sharply-dressed teenagers promenade back and forth and crowds gather outside the cinemas in noisy clusters that keep reforming as friends catch sight of each other.

When I suggested that we sit in the centre of the square, the two Palestinians seemed uneasy. Looking around, I realized that although Tel Aviv employs 20,000 Arab migrant workers, according to official sources, none of them seemed to be here. Still, it was hard to be sure. Black hair, a white teeshirt, jeans and sneakers are as likely to denote an Iraqi Jew as a

Palestinian, and some Polish Jews resemble Arabs in skin colour and semitic features after years in the Mediterranean.

The armed guards leaning against the square's borders with apparent langour, however, clearly knew the difference. Ceaselessly scanning the crowd, their eyes would periodically alight on someone, causing them to jump into action. They would walk up to the man with the left hand outstretched for his identity papers. A quick glance and he was waved on or, in one case, taken away.

An Israeli army officer once told me he could spot young Palestinians since their bodies, although muscular from manual work, do not show the well-fed sturdiness of Israelis. School sports and para-military training, followed by three years in the army, engender a heavy walk that starts from a strong broad neck. Healthy food, coupled with good dental care, makes for even, white teeth. There are no school gyms or dentists in the refugee camps of the West Bank or Gaza.

What the guards were looking for were not just terrorists but also illegals, Palestinians from the occupied territories spending the night in town without a permit. The permits are rarely given, but being caught without one is a criminal offence leading to arrest, a court case and a high fine. The restriction is officially based on security grounds, but since the same Palestinians can move around freely in the daytime, it is hard to explain.

In the end, we opted for Jaffa. Sitting in a small café surrounded by old Arab houses whose arched windows had been boarded up to create the rectangular shapes appealing to their oriental Jewish inhabitants, Ahmed and I swapped news about our families. Khalil revealed that he was engaged but unsure when he would marry. "What kind of husband can he be, sleeping five nights a week in his managers' spare flat with eight other men because there is no work in the camp?", Ahmed asked me.

"It'll be all right. Things will get easier when we have a state of our own", said Khalil with an embarrassed grin. I realized I had heard the phrase before. A character in *Fiddler on the Roof*, a musical based on the lives of Russian Jews at the turn of the century, had said a very similar thing . . .

UP AGAINST THE WIRE IN CANADA

Martin Wright

The desert road from Cairo to the Israeli border skirts the northern edge of the Sinai Peninsula and swings up towards the Gaza Strip, passing on its way two contrasting relics of the Arab–Israeli conflict.

At Qantara, just across the Suez Canal, clusters of dead tanks crouch in the scrub, some half-engulfed in shrouds of soft sand. Since the Yom Kippur war, when Israeli and Egyptian armour came together in one of the largest tank battles the world has even seen, they've sat frozen in their moment of death or abandonment, burnt out or strangely intact, embalmed by uncleared minefields. A few lie tidily in line abreast, as though knocked out while on some innocent parade. It looks and feels like an anachronism, with few reverberations into the present. Post-Camp David, sleek Israeli tour buses glide through on their way to the Pyramids.

Up the road at Rafah, it's a different story. Split down the middle when the Israelis pulled out of Sinai, checkpoints and razor wire bisect the high street. Turn off the main drag metres from the border post, follow the bumpy track towards the sea, and you'll end up in Canada. Stencilled characters on a blockhouse wall confirm your arrival in Arabic and English:

"WELLCOME TO CANADA CAMP. CLEANLINESS IS NEXT TO GODLINESS."

It has the look of refugee camps everywhere: breeze block houses with corrugated roofs, plastic or iron, topped by water drums and TV aerials; power lines over muddy streets, the odd faded Palestinian flag flapping from the wires. Inside, calor gas cookers and rations of UNRWA flour, rice and oil on the concrete floors.

The sole Palestinian camp on Egyptian soil, it owes its name to a contingent of UN troops once based here. Set up in 1972 as an overflow from the crowded Rafah camp, this living relic passed into Egyptian control with the Israeli pullout 10 years later. At a stroke, families and friends were divided, and few of the 7,000 residents gain permission to cross the line. Those who do find it hard to cross back.

The day we arrived, a chill January wind was blowing sheets of rain in from the sea, turning the alleyways into mudslides. Inside, we're awash with traditional Arab hospitality; feasting till we're fit to burst on rice, meat and vegetables. Over mint tea and coffee, four generations of camp residents crowd in to squat on rugs, cushions and foam mattresses, keen to talk politics with the English visitors. The older ones remember a youth spent in Jaffa or some of the other coastal towns of what was then Palestine. For the vast majority, though, the refugee camp is the only life they've known.

Incongruously, we talk over the background of a Hebrew chat-show on Israeli Television, emanating from the set in the corner of the room. "It's more honest than the Egyptian channels", explains Mahmoud, one of the camp dwellers. "At least it tells us a bit about the *intifada*." "Most of us would rather be on the Israeli side of the border", adds Mahmoud's father. "It's our home there, even if it is under occupation."

There's little love lost between the residents of Canada and the Egyptian authorities, who, beneath their pro-PLO rhetoric, are wary of any overt support for the uprising across the wire. Egyptian Army jeeps prowl periodically up and down the streets, and when we venture out for a "grand tour", several chubby secret service men with absurd, presumably deliberately conspicuous, bulges under their jackets, peer unpleasantly at us from their Peugeot. Camp residents are sporadically picked up for interrogation; a few expelled from Egypt altogether, into some stateless future.

The authorities are particularly keen to guard against any repeat of the incident in 1988, when three men from the camp infiltrated into Israel and hijacked a bus travelling to the Dimona nuclear power plant. At the three corners of the camp stand thin metal poles, sunk in concrete and crowned with a shallow steel bowl—quirky memorial braziers to the three guerrillas killed in the raid.

On the Israeli side of the wire lies a 50 metre stretch of open ground, dotted with watchtowers, floodlights and Stars of David—the occasional target of enthusiastic, if optimistic, stone-throwing by the camp children. Mahmoud and his friend lead us up to the line and negotiate permission with an Egyptian soldier for us to take photos. Perched in his watchtower, an Israeli border guard watches sullenly as we aim our cameras at him through the wire.

On seeing that the visitors include two women, the Egyptian soldier's mates shout down from their blockhouse, invite us in for tea, and engage in animated banter with the two Palestinians. The commotion draws the attention of a jeepload of Israeli soldiers bouncing along on the other side of the wire, who throw in a few of their own choice comments, grinning broadly at the women.

For a few brief seconds, Egyptian, Israeli and Palestinian are thrown together in the same tease. Everyone's laughing. Just 100 metres up the line, their three flags flap damply in the rain, within just a stone's throw of each other.

1. THE PALESTINIAN DIMENSION
David McDowall

The *intifada* (uprising) has dramatically changed the dimensions of the Palestine question. At the international level it has created a political momentum which cannot be ignored, sharply contrasting with the failure of the international "peace process" to achieve anything remotely similar. Within the Palestinian movement it has achieved an unprecedented level of unity. Inside Israel it has provoked a more serious debate concerning the future of the territories than hitherto, with an increasing polarization of Israeli opinion as the need for a decision grows ever closer.

Even the USA, unable to ignore the uprising, made repeated attempts during the course of 1988 to revive its flagging Jordanian option. But in July 1988, King Hussein of Jordan decided to relinquish sovereignty over the West Bank as he, too, accepted there could no longer be a realistic hope of the West Bank ever accepting a return to Jordanian rule.

The unanticipated success of the uprising has given the PLO its most important political card, one which has left it feeling strong enough to make other concessions long called for by the West but which it had previously felt too weak to make unambiguously. At the 19th PNC in Algiers in November 1988, the PLO accepted UN Security Council Resolution 242 more explicitly than hitherto. Furthermore, it declared the independence of the State of Palestine according to UN Partition Resolution 181 of 1947. These developments persuaded the member states of the European Community to open ministerial level discussions with the PLO as representative of the Palestinian people, followed more reluctantly by the United States which made it clear that talks with the PLO would remain contingent on its continued "good behaviour".

For Israel and the United States, neither of which want to see the creation of a Palestinian state, the most important means of preventing further slippage in their respective positions on the Palestine question lies in bringing the uprising to an end. Both governments hold out the prospect of political progress for the Palestinians only once there is an end, or at least a dramatic decline, in the level of disorder. Although it is possible that the United States government genuinely intends political progress, presumably along the lines of the autonomy proposals contained in the Camp David Accords, most Palestinians believe, probably rightly, that since their only political gains have resulted from Israel's inability to suppress the uprising, any suspension of it would also spell a halt to their long march towards independence.

Here lies the central dilemma for the Palestinian people: how best to achieve their goal of an independent state in Palestine. It is on this question that the Palestinians face a threat greater than Israeli subjugation or hostile American machinations; the danger of a return to the disunity that has plagued the national movement both inside and outside the territories, intermittently since 1967 and most notably during the first half of the 1980s.

Ever since the meteoric growth of the Palestinian armed struggle in the late 1960s, there have been fundamental differences of opinion among the different political constituents of the PLO concerning the means whereby Palestine can be recovered.

At an ideological level there has always been a divide between the mainstream organisation, *Fatah*, which seeks to achieve a state in part or all of Palestine, and the more radical groups which see the continued existence of Zionism as fundamentally inimical with their own view of democracy in all Palestine, and see the Arab regimes as part of their problem rather than—as *Fatah* has tended to see them—as allies in finding a solution.

In practice, *Fatah*, which controls the PLO leadership, is more willing to compromise with both Israel and the United States in order to win back the occupied territories than are the PFLP, the DFLP or the Palestine Communist Party (PCP), all of which have serious reservations concerning this willingness to strike a deal. They remember that in 1978 the PLO leadership wanted to explore the autonomy provisions of the Camp David Accords and was only dissuaded from doing so by the adamant rejection of them by the putative beneficiaries, the inhabitants of the territories themselves.

Furthermore, there is residual distrust of the way in which *Fatah* has tried to control developments and diplomacy. Following Camp David, a National Guidance Committee (NGC) was established in the territories, composed of various leading Palestinians but with an undeniably leftist hue. *Fatah* did not like this and wanted to exert direct control. Both the PFLP and the DFLP supported the NGC in its independence, partly because they saw it as a counter-weight to *Fatah*. When Israel crushed the NGC, *Fatah* was not particularly sorry. Indeed, it co-operated with the Jordanian authorities in providing financial support to those Palestinians who accepted either *Fatah*'s or Jordan's external direction, while witholding such help from

NGC supporters. At the time, these conflicts—and the open split with the PLO from 1983–6—created deep bitterness within the Palestinian movement. With the *intifada*, the Palestinians were able to put these divisions behind them.

Most Palestinians fear that any hesitation over the next step towards liberation opens the door to another potential round of feuding between the factions. More than anything else, the inhabitants of the territories are anxious not to let this happen.

This concern raises another important feature of the uprising, the way in which the Palestinian movement's centre of gravity has shifted away from the PLO headquarters to the more shadowy leadership of the Unified National Leadership of the Uprising (UNLU). Although UNLU is part of the PLO, and has publicly acknowledged the *leadership* of the PLO, the reality is more complex. UNLU is composed of leaders of the *Fatah*, DFLP, PFLP, and Communist Party cadres in the territories. To that extent they know and are loyal to the external leadership. But they are also aware that they are now in the driving seat, and that the uprising to which they give leadership is the essential instrument whereby freedom is likely to be attained. Furthermore, most of these leaders know that they understand the struggle they are waging against the occupier and against Jordan a good deal better than does the PLO leadership in Tunis.

As one might guess, after 20 years of effort to prevent local initiatives unless these were firmly subordinated to external PLO guidance, the PLO leadership has mixed feelings concerning UNLU's power. It cannot possibly want an end to the uprising, its sole source of power today after years of impotence, but it must feel ambivalent about UNLU's authority and power concerning events in the occupied territories. Consequently, with regard to the balance within the Palestinian movement, the PLO is bound to welcome diplomatic developments which put it, rather than UNLU, back in the driving seat.

Recognizing that it is by international diplomacy that the right to self-determination may well be realized, the United Leadership looks forward to fruitful negotiations by the PLO with Israel and the super-powers. But it will wish to continue to remind the PLO of realities on the ground, and also provide a failsafe mechanism which will prevent the PLO leadership from offering too much in return for too little. In this respect it is important to note something that has not been adequately recognized outside the territories, that the PLO leadership is probably *more* accommodating in practice than are the actual inhabitants of the territories who seek an end to occupation. This, at least, was the finding of a survey conducted before the commencement of the uprising, in 1986.[1]

Nor has UNLU been frightened of cautioning the PLO leadership publicly. When King Hussein relinquished his claim to the West Bank, it published a communiqué in which it said "the PLO outside the territories should not 'fill the gap' left by Jordan by duplicating its work, which was based on the principle of patronage through corruption. The challenge is to find ways to support the existing popular structures so that they can better continue the struggle". No such warning would have been published had UNLU not harboured fears concerning the PLO leadership's propensity for patronage already experienced since 1978. When Arafat met King Hussein and President Mubarak of Egypt in Aqaba in October 1988 amid reports of negotiations for a Palestinian–Jordanian confederation, UNLU was quick to warn that "when the Palestinian National Movement is increasingly united around clear, unambiguous political proposals, rumours of confederation negotiations are worrying and confusing".

The shift in power is partly geographical—from outside to inside the territories—but it is also generational. The PLO leadership is composed of men in their 50s and 60s, who remember the catastrophe of 1948 and who responded to the call of Arab nationalism. By Palestinian standards they are comparatively old men, with old fashioned views on the struggle. Their contemporaries inside the occupied territories, personified by the pro-PLO mayors elected in 1976, have all been eclipsed by the *shabab*, the young men. Over half the population of the territories is under 20, with no memory of life before the occupation nor any memory of the heyday of Arab nationalism. All they know is the impotence of the Arab world or even the PLO to regain Palestine. Forty years younger than the external leadership, their outlook is quite different. As one Palestinian journalist, Daoud Kuttab, wrote six months before the outbreak of the uprising:

"These young people who have grown up under Israeli occupation take a much more radical approach than the PLO leadership. Having grown up under the nose of the Israeli war machine, young Palestinians have come to the conclusion that, in the world they inhabit, might is right and the only way to survive and flourish is to be strong and violent. Diplomatic missions and political initiatives don't mean anything to these young people who have seen only more oppression as Israel speaks of

[1] M. Shadid and J. Selzer, "Political attitudes of Palestinians in the West Bank and Gaza Strip", *Middle East Journal*, Winter 1988, vol. 42, no. 1.

peace. Although for the present time this generation has strong feelings for the PLO and its chairman, Yasser Arafat, they have grown impatient with the niceties of political diplomacy".[2]

In view of these intricacies, it must be anticipated that Israel and the USA will, so long as self-determination remains the uprising's goal and so long as these two governments remain opposed to it, do their best to bring the PLO leadership to settle for significantly less or to produce a split in Palestinian ranks by offering enough to draw *Fatah*, but insufficient for the DFLP, PFLP and the Communists.

Such a split might be catastrophic for the present PLO leadership, and for the short and medium term prospects for peace. But in the longer term, the span of decades rather than months or years will not avert the growth of the Palestinian independence movement.

The PLO leadership is aware of the dangers it runs. On the one hand it must not give way too easily to American pressure. On the other, if it is unable to participate as the negotiating organ of the Palestinian people, the balance of authority will continue to shift from the PLO Headquarters in Tunis to the leadership on the ground. That is why it is anxious to transform the physical actions of the uprising into solid political developments negotiated by itself. The longer it is unable to play a productive diplomatic role, the less authority it will command among the Palestinian people.

After the initial, but clearly unenthusiastic agreement of the US Administration to parley with the PLO, by the spring of 1989 there was a growing sense of frustration at the slow and minimalist response of the United States. There remains a considerable danger that if the United States drags its feet, the accommodationist wing of the PLO, which has worked for a negotiated settlement under the aegis of an international conference, may well be eclipsed by those who believe that Israel will only relinquish the occupied territories once it is persuaded that hanging onto them has become an intolerable burden.

At the moment the constituent members of the PLO are prepared to give the leadership the benefit of the doubt, and allow it to pursue its diplomatic policy. So also is the United National Leadership. But the accommodationist policy is on trial. This was made clear by the PFLP leadership at the 19th PNC, when it opposed acceptance of Resolution 242, but agreed not to obstruct the initiative. However, the PLO leadership knows that this tolerance remains contingent on its own ability to demonstrate that concessions by the Palestinians have produced concessions from the United States. In the absence of results, the

[2] *Al Fajr English Weekly*, 31 May 1987.

DFLP and Communists are likely to follow the PFLP position. More seriously, the PLO leadership must take account of the natural impatience of the *shabab*, the youth of the territories, at the meagre gains achieved by diplomacy over the years and their disbelief in American sincerity. As Kuttab warned, "if they (the *shabab*) see that the PLO's political initiatives are producing no results, they will force the PLO into a more radical posture or else they will go looking for a more radical leadership within the PLO".[3] It hardly needs saying that growing frustration at the lack of diplomatic progress will, in any case, encourage an intensification of the *intifada*.

If the PLO leadership feels compelled to retreat because of the failure of the USA to respond adequately to its initiatives, it will be able to point to Resolution 242 as an increasingly pointless basis for peace. In the first place, the USA, so long as it refuses to accept Palestinian statehood, has no legitimate sovereign state to which the West Bank can be returned (in view of King Hussein's renunciation of it). The PLO can also point to Israel's illegal settlements and progressive seizure of land, and its present government's claim that Samaria, Judaea and Gaza are all inalienable parts of *Eretz Yisrael* which cannot be surrendered, as evidence that while the PLO is required to accept Resolution 242, Israel by contrast does not accept its meaning as understood by the Security Council.

In the meantime, critically important developments will continue to make Israel's position progressively weaker. Inside the occupied territories, the inexorable increase of the population will make the territories harder to govern. At a crude demographic level, the present estimated population of the West Bank and Gaza Strip, probably of the order of 1 million and 650,000 respectively in 1988, is likely to exceed 1.5 million and 1 million by the turn of the century.

But it is not merely a matter of exercising law and order. The services which were already dangerously inadequate in 1988 are destined to become even more so. Take the question of schooling. Between 1988 and the end of the century the school population in the West Bank will increase by roughly 50 per cent, and by roughly 60 per cent in Gaza. Poor teacher–student ratios, 1:28 in government schools, 1:30 in UNRWA ones, will deteriorate further, inviting a collapse in the system.

Meanwhile, in order merely to keep pace with school leavers, the economy must create an average of 7,000 new jobs a year. The lack of economic growth under the occupation has already meant that there is little incentive to continue schooling, and that work for over a third of the work force can only be found

[3] *Al Fajr English Weekly*, 31 May 1987.

inside Israel. The inexorable growth of an unemployed or deeply dissatisfied workforce will continue to undermine the efforts of the authorities to maintain law and order.

One further point may be made on the question of population growth, and the way in which this makes the territories increasingly ungovernable, whether by Israel or some future Palestinian authority. This is the question of population density in Gaza. In 1988 the Gaza Strip was the most densely populated territory in the world, with approximately 1,500 persons per square kilometre, rivalling Hong Kong but without any of the latter's infrastructural attributes. By the turn of the century its density will be nearly 2,600 persons per square kilometre. As time ticks away virtually nothing is done about this growing crisis.

Population density is also oppressive at the domestic level. Forty nine per cent of the West Bank and 45 per cent of the Gaza Strip live at a density of seven persons per household. These percentages are rising inexorably upwards. Merely to cater for the increase of population between 1988 and the end of the century requires the construction of 90,000 new homes. Yet building permits continue to be difficult to obtain on account of Israeli reluctance (as with its own Palestinian citizens in Galilee) to allow the Palestinians to strengthen their physical presence on the land through construction. But the result, of course, is that the Palestinians live with what one might describe as the pressure cooker effect, physical at first but in the end political in its impact.

Two other factors will strengthen the hand of the Palestinian national movement if Israel continues to resist a settlement acceptable to it. The first important consideration is the growing politicization and proportional growth of Israel's own Palestinian citizens living mainly in the Galilee. In the mid-1970s the Arab Israelis rejoiced at the growth of Palestinian nationalism in the occupied territories and began, themselves, to feel that they, too, should be described as Palestinian, rather than Arab. Today this feeling has become much stronger, partly as a result of the uprising but also because members of the younger generation wish to express their Palestinian identity more strongly than their parents dared to.

This does not mean that Israeli Palestinians are suddenly going to repudiate their Israeli citizenship and unite with the territories. Most Israeli Palestinians still accept that their future is as Israeli citizens, and some have ambivalence about what their Palestinian identity means in practice. Forty years of incorporation in the Jewish State means that they are now culturally different from Palestinians east of the 1949 Armistice Line, frequently being more fluent on paper in Hebrew than in Arabic. They occupy an uncomfortable middle culture, feeling Arab in Tel Aviv but Israeli in Nablus.

However, they are clear about two issues, the right of the PLO to create a Palestinian state in the territories, and their own right to functional equality, particularly in terms of political and economic power, within Israel. Every day that Israel drags its feet on these issues increases the possibility that Palestinians both sides of the 1949 Armistice Line will begin to consider a common political destiny. Such a development would pose a far greater threat to the Jewish State than the present uprising. Already, in spite of repeated state efforts to settle Jews, Palestinians have become a growing majority in the Northern District (the whole area north of a line from the northern edge of Haifa to the north-west tip of the West Bank), rising to 50 per cent in 1985 and set to become about 60 per cent by the end of the century. If these Palestinians despaired of achieving equality inside Israel and turned to ideas of secession, it would present an awkward complication to an accommodationist PLO leadership, willing to strike a deal with Israel (as the present leadership seems to be) to recover no more than the occupied territories. The PLO might find the desire of Israeli Palestinians to throw in their lot with the national liberation struggle deeply embarrassing since it would probably make further negotiations with Israel impossible.

The second factor is the growing Palestine refugee problem, now that it is beyond doubt that they will not assimilate into their host countries as originally anticipated. It has always been argued by Israel that the refugee problem is an Arab responsibility. Whether or not one accepts this view, neither Israel nor the PLO will be able to transact a durable settlement which does not address the problem adequately. The Palestine refugees currently in Lebanon have no future there. By the end of the 1980s they numbered some 300,000, but by the turn of the century they will number almost 400,000 unless there is substantial migration or a dramatic fall in their birth rate. Where will they find a safe haven? They will naturally continue to dream of Galilee and the coastal cities of Haifa and Acre, from which their parents or grandparents fled.

The largest number of refugees live in Jordan. They constitute approximately 40 per cent of Jordan's East Bank population, some 900,000 in 1988. In the event of the physical establishment of a Palestinian state, King Hussein will want a substantial proportion—perhaps half—of these refugees to leave for two reasons. He cannot look forward to the prospect of 40 per cent of his subjects directing their loyalty to the Palestinian state across the river, rather than to the Hashemite Crown. Furthermore, the economy of Jordan over the past 20 years has been sustained by two main sources, the remittances of Jordanian workers in the Gulf, and the large subsidies from the West and from pro-Western Arab states to ensure Jordan's ability to withstand the rigours of the Arab–Israeli conflict. With the downturn in the Gulf economy since the mid-1980s, Jordan's own economy has declined. If the West's subsidies came to an end, Jordan's economic and therefore political stability would be in question. Hussein will want a smaller and more loyal population, and that means encouraging Palestinians to cross the river.

It is difficult to see how the occupied territories could absorb another million or so people from Jordan and Lebanon, given the absence of economic infrastructure and the already acutely overcrowded conditions of Gaza.

One final point should be made about the refugees. The passion with which the younger generation holds the right to return is a mirror image of the Zionist zeal of young Jews 50 years ago. If the PLO cannot satisfy this claim there is a real danger that a new movement for the refugee right of return will grow, and that it will find support not only among refugees now outside Palestine but also in the crowded camps of Gaza, even after the establishment of a Palestinian state. This poses a problem for the stability of any Palestinian state, let alone the durability of the kind of peace agreement which Israel may in due course seek.

Whatever happens now on the diplomatic stage, whether or not the present PLO leadership is able to entice Israel to the negotiating table and retain the loyalty (or at least co-operation) of its Palestinian critics, the fundamental challenge posed by the uprising will not go away. A historical process is now under way. From its first burst of fury in December 1987, the people of the *intifada* have learnt how to organize and defend themselves against the occupier. The process is one of discovery: of individual and community dignity, and of the ways in which the community can gather together its potential energy and organize it in a truly popular way. In other words, what is currently being waged against Israel is a people's war.

How precisely it will unfold may be impossible to say, but in order to understand the developing dynamics of the Palestinian–Israeli struggle, the observer's eye should focus less on the policies of the superpowers, the PLO leaders or the Israeli government, and more on the changing balance between aspiration and pragmatism that directs the behaviour of the two communities which inhabit the land of Palestine.

2. THE ISRAELI DIMENSION

Noah Lucas

In the general election of Autumn 1988, any casual or indeed seasoned observer of Israeli politics could have been forgiven for thinking that the essential issue of the campaign was that of Israel's relations with the Palestinians. The media uniformly interpreted the election as presenting a vital choice of strategies to settle the conflict. Yet as soon as the votes were counted the Prime Minister on behalf of *Likud*, vied with the leaders of Labour in seeking to tempt the ultra-religious politicians into a coalition government on terms in which the Palestinian question was virtually ignored.

In these negotiations the question, "Who is a Jew?", replaced "What is a Palestinian?" at the top of the agenda. When *Likud* failed after several weeks of bargaining to reach an agreement with the religious parties, it abruptly turned to Labour. In record time, they agreed to form a national unity government which placed *both* the Palestinian question and the issue of Jewish identity on the back burner.

The two key issues governing the self-definition of the Jewish state, its relations with the Palestinians and the Arab world on the one hand, and with Judaism and Diaspora Jewry on the other, were simply dropped like hot potatoes, and the new government got on with the business of trying to contain the Palestinian uprising and fending off economic recession.

The crisis seizing Israeli society has its roots a century deep in the history and pre-history of the state. Israel is the product of a revolutionary movement dedicated to the creation of a new man, the secular-Jewish Israeli national, out of what appeared to be the crumbling old Jewish tradition of absolute religious devotion. The Zionist revolutionary background of Israel, involving as it did the creation of a modern Jewish order instead of passive acceptance of an inherited status of indignity, compels it constantly to formulate and reformulate the nature of Israeli national identity. This in turn forces the state to elaborate an ideology relating the Israeli nation both to Jewry abroad and to the Arabs, a necessity which generates poignant contradictions and brings them to the surface of public life. Moreover, given the small scale of the country and its tight-knit institutions there is a systemic interlinking of diverse problems. Hence the crisis is chronic, becoming acute from time to time as a result of rapid changes occurring in parts of the system.

Israel's current wave of crisis presents the paradox of polarization within national unity. As they did in 1984, the two major parties joined at the end of 1988 in a national government based, in effect, on evasion of the most important issues on which the country and the political parties are deeply divided. This was possible because, on the Palestinian question, *Likud* and Labour each preferred the *status quo* to the implementation of the other's programme, while on the Jewish religious issues they both preferred the *status quo* to accommodating the extreme demands of the religious parties. The apparent unity is thus a reflection of deadlock in a tug of war rather than an equilibrium of forces conducive to progressive decision-making.

Does this mean that Israel is bound to have weak, indecisive government for the foreseeable future? More likely, an Israeli government which cannot decide its response to important changes beyond its control will support the *status quo* with even more vigorous decisiveness. Stronger, united government investing ever greater resources and energies in holding back the tide of change is more likely to be the result, than weakness and indecision in government reflecting the divisions of the society. Certainly as long as American support is maintained, and probably even if it is not, Israel will summon a muscular obduracy in resisting any shift in direction which is not endorsed by a wide consensus. Israel is capable of seething in turmoil and straining in deadlock for years, at the cost of an insidious deterioration in the quality of life, before bending to the wind of unwelcome change. Such is the resilience of the people and the strength of patriotic conviction within each camp, that there is no break in sight in this battle of wills, so it should not be thought that pressure exerted by the forces of change, whether internal, Palestinian, or external, will in the near future determine the outcome.

The Palestinian uprising has disturbed the equilibrium that was beginning to form within the general public around the notion that the boundaries of the state would eventually stabilize on the River Jordan. The relatively passive and quiescent attitude of the older generation of Arabs, under military occupation since 1967, had led the country to believe that Israeli rule was capable of sustaining co-existence between the two peoples. The political leaders fed this illusion by maintaining the conviction that Israel's conflicts with the Arab world could be settled with the states with which it had been at war, and that the Palestinian issue derived from this and could be dissolved within any such settlement.

Under Labour leadership from 1967–1977, confusion reigned in Israel over the extent of its claims. Prime Ministers Levi Eshkol, Golda Meir and Itzhak Rabin all sought to postpone any resolution of the Palestinian issue, which they thought would generate a Jewish civil war. They were able to do this as long as Arab policies kept negotiations and peace off the agenda. In 1977, with the election of a *Likud* government under Menahem Begin and the launching of President Sadat's grand peace initiative, a trade-off was contrived in which Israel returned the Sinai peninsula to Egypt and a bilateral peace was achieved between them, while the continuation of the peace-making process involving the Palestinians was effectively made conditional on recognition of ultimate Israeli sovereignty over all the other occupied territories. Israel's new claim to sovereignty in all the land west of the Jordan, although asserted by Prime Minister Begin upon his election in 1977, was not supported by the majority of the public, but it succeeded in foiling further negotiations on a settlement, and fostered a climate in which hard-line nationalism flourished in Israel.

The *Likud* government, first under Prime Minister Begin and then continuing under the leadership of Itzhak Shamir, habitually exploited a new wave of religious emotional fervour to enhance the legitimacy of Israel's national aggrandizement. Ironically, after two generations in which religious Jewry fought a losing battle against territorial nationalism under secularist auspices, many ultra-religious Jews under the spell of the events of 1967, which they regarded as miraculous, now adopted an ultra-nationalist ideology in which the issue of boundaries was placed at the very centre of Israel's national myth.

The great majority of the ultra-religious remain anti-nationalist or non-Zionist and are decidedly 'dovish'. But the movement of extremist religious settlers to Arab-populated centres on the West Bank was given a brief new spurt, with the declared intention of making it difficult, if not impossible, for Israel to withdraw from the territories. The settlement drive was rapidly played out for lack of recruits, so that the religious now comprise well below half of the puny total of some 65,000 settlers established since 1967. At any rate they did succeed in complicating any future Israeli policy of withdrawal, as they are fully expected to offer violent resistance to any such move.

The high profile of the religious settlers led to a common distortion in the assessment of their impact, accounting them disproportionately influential due to the system of proportional representation or the vagaries of coalition politics. Conventional wisdom notwithstanding, the secularists, Itzhak Shamir and Moshe Arens, Ariel Sharon, David Levy and the rest never for a moment lost control of policy, but have consistently used the religious, who have happily enough performed their assigned task in the light of their conviction that the secularists are mere pawns of divine purpose.

The fact that secular nationalists regard religion as a source of legitimacy for their policies signals the failure of secularist Zionism to cut Jewish identity free of its religious foundations. Israel is accordingly becoming more conscious of its religious roots at the very time when Jewry abroad, under the influence of Zionism and Israeli nationalism, is more prone to rediscover its Jewish identity and define its political interests along secular channels. Jewry abroad is diverging in its development from the close affinity for Israeli concerns which has marked it for some decades. World Jewry is less and less readily falling in line behind Israeli commitments in which the prospect of peace with the Arabs recedes further and further from reality. At the same time Jewry abroad, especially pluralistic American Jewry, is increasingly embarrassed by Israel's tendency to claim religious authority for acts of policy towards the Palestinians in which ancient stones and monuments are held more significant than living interests. Not that Jewish support for Israel is about to collapse. However, there is every likelihood that if the Arab population should become a majority and the democratic character of the state is seen to fail, that it will cease to have the emotional significance for Jewry that it has held since the Nazi holocaust. Jewry abroad is ineluctably involved in the question of Jewish–Palestinian relations, and is likely from its vantage point to draw different conclusions from the Israelis about the best way to achieve a resolution.

Israeli diplomatic doctrine since 1977 continued to hold the settlement of the Palestinian issue conditional on agreement with the Arab states, and especially Jordan. In renouncing responsibility for the West Bank at the end of July 1988, King Hussein put paid to this myth. Hussein's act made clear what had in fact been the case since the occupation of 1967, that the conflict was at heart one between communities rather than states.

Labour's dependency on the Jordanian factor was greater than *Likud*'s, given its wish to return territory to Jordanian sovereignty. *Likud* theoretically stood for Jordanian abdication in any case, but this in conjunction with its acceptance and recognition of Israeli sovereignty in the territories. *Likud*'s diplomatic posture was shaken when the Palestinians ceased to play the part assigned to them, as rejectionists. No less challenging to Israel than the uprising was the new peace diplomacy of the PLO, led from the Palestinian Diaspora.

The "unity" government formed at the end of 1988 did undertake to prepare a new peace plan of its own both to counter the unaccustomed diplomacy of the PLO and to satisfy the United States that Israel would sustain some movement towards peace, notwithstanding the withdrawal of King Hussein, its favoured interlocutor. But it was clear enough that little more than public relations peace rhetoric would emerge, since there never was any chance that a *Likud*-led government would consider yielding an inch of occupied territory to Palestinian claims. So far as the Palestinians were concerned, as caustically pointed out by Abba Eban, Israel would not take "yes" for an answer.

In choosing not to go into opposition on the issue of peace, Labour presumably hoped for a breathing space to enable it to rescue the labour-owned sector of the economy from imminent bankruptcy. It was as though Labour renounced its pretensions in foreign affairs in return for the economic portfolios in government. But the pressure on it was heightened in July 1989 when the *Likud* party's central committee solemnly issued a resolution purporting to surround the government's "peace initiative" with pre-conditions sufficient to ensure that it could not initiate any process whatever except intensification of the leadership struggles within both parties.

In effect, the *Likud* forum, chaired by Prime Minister Shamir's persistent rival Ariel Sharon, called on the Israeli government to remove from its proposal for elections on the West Bank all the ambiguities and vagueness of phraseology which had enabled Labour to remain in the government without total loss of dignity. In snatching its fig-leaf Sharon compelled Labour to face the stark choice of staying in the government and losing all credibility as a party committed to peace, or going into opposition in the knowledge that it might remain out of power for a generation and fall apart as a historic party.

Since his demotion from the Ministry of Defence following the Lebanon debacle, Ariel Sharon, now in government as Minister for Trade and Industry, has struggled to rebuild his political fortunes, working closely with David Levy, the Vice-Premier, to harass the Shamir–Moshe Arens axis of the party leadership. That they have chosen to do so from the right wing reflects their judgement of where the wind blows, rather than any ideological nuance of difference. The ploy at the central committee in which Sharon humiliated Shamir both as Prime Minister and party leader may so rankle that Shamir may well seek to bury the hatchet with Levy at whatever cost and fire Sharon from the government. Not that Sharon could be expected to go quietly, but bereft of a base in the government and a majority in the party, for which he depends on Levy, Sharon's prospects as a challenger for the top leadership would be greatly diminished. Although Sharon is undoubtedly an adventurer and to that extent a man of special danger to the Arabs, he is more flexible ideologically than either Shamir or his heir-presumptive, Foreign Minister Arens. It is unlikely therefore that the outcome of the leadership rivalries in *Likud* would make much difference to the party's policy.

The Minister of Defence, Itzhak Rabin, the kingpin of the *Likud*–Labour alliance, absorbs the pressures of the uprising while serving Shamir's purpose in keeping Sharon at a good distance from the post he hankers after, and also provides a focus for those in Labour who most wish to remain in government. Judging by past form, the odds must be that Labour will stay in government, after prolonged soul-searching at all levels of the organization reveals that it is split on the issues of peace as on those of leadership. It will prefer not to hold an early election, and would rather postpone the denouement of its own leadership struggle.

Under the 10 years of Labour government after the 1967 war the Allon Plan was unofficially adopted, in which strategic settlements were established in the outer, sparsely populated areas of the West Bank. It is among these settlers, associated with the socialist sector of the *kibbutz* movement, together with the Moshav co-operative movement, that there is greatest reluctance to support Labour's official programme of substantial withdrawal from the territories. In the absence of peace moves, the divisions within Labour were never forced to a final test. In the context of the new PLO diplomacy of peace-making, Labour may be pressed to a showdown, and the leadership struggle within the coming generation may well form around the Palestinian issue. In the interim, as a stop-gap measure, the party might well sacrifice four-time loser Peres and replace him with Rabin as leader, if that is the price of choosing to remain in government as a junior partner to *Likud*.

In the longer run, if the Palestinians maintain their pressure and sustain their desire for a settlement based on a two-state blueprint, Labour may fall apart, with those favouring major withdrawal from the territories pushed out to join the left-wing opposition groups, *Mapam* and the Civil Rights Movement (*Ratz*) to form the nucleus of a "peace front". The Palestinian strategy of peace and recognition came too late to affect the last election in Israel. If the strategy holds good it may succeed in reshaping the whole pattern of Israeli politics around the single issue. Be that as it may, it is for some time to come not on the fringes but in the centre ground of the main parties, albeit now further to the right than 10 years ago, that the crucial contest for the soul of the country is joined. At best, while it marks time, Labour can claim that its continuation in government is essential to forestall an economic collapse with inflation raging at over 500% per year, such as had characterized the last period of *Likud* rule free of the restraining hand of Labour.

When they are twinned in harness the two major parties hold each other to some extent in check, but this is not to say that their respective postures are completely symmetrical. While the national unity arrangement lasts, Labour has to make the greater sacrifice of principle, and conform to a policy in government much closer to the *Likud*'s preferred approach than to its own desires. This is because Labour knows that it cannot deliver its programme of territorial concessions, not only because its own supporters are divided on the issue and public opinion is dubious, but because the right-wing opposition would undoubtedly use every means including violence to thwart it.

The *Likud*, by contrast, as in the case of the negotiated treaty with Egypt a decade ago, acquires political leverage in the sure knowledge that it can rely on Labour to support any forward diplomacy it sponsors. Thus the crux of *immobilisme* is the fact that although only a government of right-wing tendency can wield the political clout needed to effect any significant Israeli concessions to the Palestinians, any government of this ideological hue will adamantly oppose making such concessions on the West Bank.

Likud and Labour are separated distinctly by their different attitudes to the territories occupied in 1967. *Likud* asks, in effect: where and when and how must diplomacy and/or *war*, including if need be civil war, be waged in order to secure for all time Israel's hold on Judaea and Samaria? In Labour's divided ranks the hawks pose a different question: what is the maximum territory that Israel can hold without detriment to its security?, while Labour doves ask: what is the minimum territory that need be held for security? Although Labour starts, like *Likud*, from the possibly false inherited assumption that the territories were a political and military asset, at any rate its approach allows room for the follow-up question: what Israeli territorial concessions on the West Bank consistent with security might help to bring about a peace settlement with the Palestinians and the Arab world at large? *Likud*'s ideological vocabulary cannot accommodate such a question, and hence its concept of concession in the occupied territories is limited strictly to palliative formulae on the model of "personal autonomy", which it is assumed can be made operable under Israeli sovereignty. The two parties are therefore not engaged in a debate based on common assumptions, but are essentially at cross purposes. This is not to say that *Likud* does not want peace at all, or to imply that Labour is willing to take greater risks for peace.

Likud does not in fact believe that peace with the Palestinians is possible for the foreseeable future, nor that concessions in the form of return of some or all of the occupied territories to Arab sovereignty would bring peace a day nearer. On the contrary, to yield territory would simply force Israel to fight on worse terms. Partition of the country, as resulting from the war and formalized in the armistice agreements of 1948–1949, was not and is not accepted by *Likud*. In the *Likud* view, peace will ensue only when the Palestinians come to realize that Israel is there to stay in all of Palestine west of the River Jordan; that is, when the Palestinians submit to Israel's claims. That is the peace *Likud* desires and believes to be the only one possible, or which may become possible with the passage of time, provided Israel stands firm, shows its strength, and makes its aim absolutely clear.

As for Labour, in showing willingness to trade territory for peace, it does not feel that it is increasing the risks to Israel, but rather that it reduces the danger, since it believes that holding all the territories incurs greater risks than relinquishing some of them. This view is based primarily on the fear that within a generation the Arabs under Israeli control will outnumber the Jewish population.

Likud's policy derives from an absolute doctrine of the dominant *Herut* wing of the party, according to which the historic claim to the "Land of Israel" applies to all of it, and any partition undermines its claim to the part retained. While the *Likud* argues from notions of right rather than security, it is clear that its ideology subsumes security, on the grounds that the security of Israel requires holding on to all land which is part of Israel. Labour, on the other hand, while asserting a moral right to the land as an abstract principle, considers the actual borders to be a product of political circumstance, and regards partition as a necessary and therefore acceptable historical compromise.

The growth of the Arab population under Israel's control, known familiarly as the "demographic problem", was initially seen by *Likud* as a minor issue so long as the Jews retained political power. Ironically enough, largely as a result of Labour propaganda harping on the demographic problem, there is a groundswell of opinion, sounded by extremist right-wing parties in opposition but echoing also in the *Likud* ranks, which recognizes the validity of Labour's analysis portending the destruction of either the Jewish or the democratic character of the state if the occupation continues. Far from concluding that there must therefore be an Israeli withdrawal from the occupied territories, the followers of this line consider that the *Arabs* must go.

Underlying the respective approaches of *Likud* and Labour are differing implications for the Israeli Arabs, the 700,000 full citizens of Israel who are resident within the borders of the old Green Line. Implicit in *Likud*'s notion of "personal autonomy" for the Arab inhabitants of the West Bank is avoidance of any need to draw territorial markers in the region, and the possibility of sustaining the writ of Israeli law among the Jewish settlers who as non-Arabs would not be affected by personal autonomy. In effect, the integration of the territories with the rest of Israel is intended and would likely ensue. Labour, preferring a territorial solution in the form of a re-partition of the land, envisages a danger to Israel's stability in that the idea of autonomy, offered to the Arabs as Arabs, could catch on within the Green Line, and undermine the loyalty and identification of Israeli Arabs with the state. From time to time during the uprising, there has been evidence of a growing Palestinian nationalist consciousness among Israeli Arabs, but not to the point at which their status as a minority within Israel has become intolerable. The installation of Palestinian autonomy on the West Bank could accelerate a major change, requiring a redefinition of the whole set of political relations between the two national groups. *Likud* policies have brought about a situation in which investment in the Jewish settlements in the West Bank exceed those in the Galilee region, where the Israeli Arabs have become a majority of the population. If it is the case that *Likud*, obsessed as it is with holding the territories as a matter of absolute principle, has not fully thought through the ultimate effects of its policy of creating a bi-national state on unequal terms, it is quite possible that it would react to a major disturbance of national accommodation by adopting the most Draconian measures, by whatever name, which could lead to extrusion of the Arabs.

The Palestinian uprising has had the effect on the Israeli policy debate of reinforcing rather than changing the views held by the two mainstream parties. The *Likud*, and those on the right generally, draw the conclusion that the uprising demonstrates the danger of allowing the Palestinians to think that they have some hope of achieving statehood; a delusion, in the *Likud* view, stimulated and nourished by the diplomacy of the Labour leaders pitched to territorial concessions. Labour, for its part, sees the uprising as conclusive proof that those territories that are heavily populated are untenable. In challenging Israeli control, the uprising has in effect psychologically restored to the map the pre-1967 borders known as the "Green Line". But while Labour willingly enough accepts the "Green Line" as a point of reference, *Likud* refuses to concede that any line implying partition has validity. In practice, the *intifada* does not therefore exert much impact on the internal balance of forces within Israel.

Some change may arise from the possible effects of the uprising on a new generation of Israelis who will exercise their vote for the first time in the next election. Those coming of age are observing that there is a considerable price to be paid for the occupation, a price that they as conscripts will be the first to pay. Until the uprising began in December 1987, it was possible for Israeli teenagers to imagine that the territories were an asset that cost little to hold. As long as the older generation of Palestinians under military rule appeared passively to accept their lot, Israeli hunger for the land was fed by possession. The younger voters, who have no memory of the "Green Line" and have known only possession of the whole land as a norm, have shown a consistent right-wing tendency from election to election.

Ideologically it is unlikely that the young generation, educated in a nationalistic syllabus, will be any less susceptible than their elders to the lure of territory that is redolent of biblical and historical mystique. Nevertheless, the price of retention, as long as resistance continues, is a price that the young conscripts will pay in unpleasant service resembling police duty and riot control rather than in military exploits endowed with public prestige. So there may be a nuance of change implicit in the balance of advantage and disadvantage as experienced by the young generation on the threshold of political maturity, albeit change which will take considerable time to work through the electoral system.

While the public is divided and deadlocked, there is evidence that the centre of gravity of public opinion may well be to the left of the government on the Palestinian issue. An opinion poll taken at the end of 1988 found that a majority of the public favoured talks with the PLO at the very moment when the new government was vehemently ruling this out. From time to time there appears similar evidence of an undertow of dovishness pulling against the conventional hawkishness that prevails on the surface. Surveys have shown again and again that the Sephardic Jews, of Middle Eastern origin, who make up the majority of the population, and are anti-Arab by reputation, are more dovish than their leaders in the *Likud*, and are not bound by the same rigid *Herut* ideology whose roots go back to the Zionism of the 1920s.

Israel's conflict with the Arabs, and in particular the direct and constant confrontation between the Jews and the Palestinians, is the intractable crucial issue whose resolution determines the fate and future of the State. Political, social and economic as well as cultural developments are all closely affected by the issue, to the extent that the very conduct of the conflict as much as its outcome fashion the personality of the society.

Under the leadership of Weizmann and Ben-Gurion, pre-state Zionism had always put practical realistic goals before romantic national visions. Zionism triumphed through its inveterate pragmatism. Briefly from 1948–1967 the partition of the land was accepted by leaders and masses. After the conquests of 1967, Israel began to lose its head, intoxicated by military victory and carried away by the euphoria of growth. Gradually as the Arabs began to accept that Israel was there to stay and that the partition of Palestine was an ineradicable fact of life, Israel moved in the other direction, savouring its new borders and recovering the sense of biblical legitimacy which, so it was thought, had once been attached to them.

There is no obvious exit from Israel's crisis. Given the dearth of leadership and statesmanship, it must be pondered whether in the course of attrition the society can escape without consuming itself.

3. PROSPECTS FOR PEACE
Roger Hardy

Has the *intifada*—the Palestinian uprising which began in December 1987—transformed the prospects for Middle East peace? It has clearly had a significant effect on Israeli and Arab politics; and it has forced the major parties to the conflict, regional and international, to rethink their attitudes to peace. But at the same time it has reinforced the essentially intractable character of the conflict—that between two peoples for one small but special piece of land.

ARAB WEAKNESS

Why the Arab states are so divided is one of the perennial questions of Middle East politics. In the 1950s and '60s, when Arab politics were dominated by President Nasser of Egypt, it was perhaps understandable for Arabs and outsiders alike to entertain the premise (or at least the possibility) of Arab unity. Several decades on, it seems more realistic to start from the premise of Arab disunity. The Arab states are sharply divided—just as most regional groupings are—between rich and poor, and between pro-Western and anti-Western; and they are also divided about Middle East peace. Some (Jordan, Syria, Lebanon) feel uncomfortably close to the problem; it scarcely impinges on others, such as Oman and Mauritania. Those with large Palestinian communities (such as Kuwait) have a bigger stake than those which don't. Above all, those with the strongest ties to the USA have the sharpest dilemma. Only a peace settlement can release them from the difficulty of maintaining a multi-faceted relationship (economic, political, military, strategic) with the power that is Israel's principal bulwark.

Arab weakness and disunity mean, among other things, that not much can be expected from the pious resolutions of Arab summits. Reducing mutual tensions and producing a modicum of working agreement is generally the most that can be achieved. The Palestinians have come to understand this quite well.

Throughout most of the 1980s—certainly since the Lebanon war of 1982—the Arab states were, by and large, more worried by Iran than by Israel. Until the Iran–Iraq ceasefire in the summer of 1988, the centre of political gravity in the Middle East was in the Gulf, not in the eastern Mediterranean. This was evident at the Arab summit in Amman in November 1987. It was the first (and so far the only) Arab summit not dominated by Palestine. Fear of Iran, and of the spread of Islamic radicalism, had pushed the Palestinians to the sidelines.

The summit's preoccupation with the Gulf was seen, in retrospect, as one of several sparks which kindled the frustration and anger of Palestinians living in the Israeli-occupied Gaza Strip and West Bank—anger which exploded the following month in the *intifada*. But though the uprising was a clear challenge to Arab inertia, it did not transform the Arab leaders overnight into zealous supporters of the Palestinian cause. It was not until a full six months after the *intifada* had begun, in June 1988, that the Arab leaders held their next summit, in Algiers. And then their backing for the uprising was distinctly lukewarm.

Again, this is surprising only to those who believe propaganda about "Arab unity" and Arab commitment to the "Arab cause" (Palestine). The essential divergence of interests between the PLO and the Arab states is not new. It is not that the Arab states do not want peace. They want peace on their own terms. Few (if any) of them want a peace settlement that would favour the PLO. Most would favour a settlement which left Palestinians under Jordanian control (or even, since this seems more likely, under an Israeli–Jordanian condominium).

Before the *intifada*, it looked as if the PLO—sorely divided after the 1982 war—was on the way to oblivion. All the Arab states needed to do was to marginalize it, starve it of funds, and hope it would (eventually) go away. The sudden eruption of the *intifada* (as unexpected in the Arab world as elsewhere) made this, at least for the time being, more difficult. But while obliging the Arab states to revive their rhetoric of support for the Palestinians (and to make, but not keep, promises of fresh funds), the *intifada* sharpened the contradiction between the interests of the Palestinians and those of the Arab states. The sight of angry young Palestinians defying well-armed Israeli soldiers frightened Arab governments as much as it electrified the Arab public. Would other young Arabs—after watching the spectacle on their television screens—imitate the Palestinian example? Riots in Algeria in the autumn of 1988, and in Jordan the following spring, seemed ominous warnings of what might be in store.

Even for the PLO chairman, Yasser Arafat, the *intifada* was double-edged. After the humiliation of the Amman summit, where he had been cold-shouldered, it enabled him to enjoy the limelight in Algiers the following year. But had he really turned the tables on his enemies and rivals? Was the summit anything more than a public relations success?

The *intifada* enabled Arafat to revive the flagging fortunes of his movement. But it also posed uncomfortable questions. The PLO existed to "liberate" Palestine. It had sought to do so through armed struggle—which, to most people, meant (or certainly included) terrorism; and through political and economic reliance on the Arab states—which meant that the Palestinians were always hostage to Arab interests and Arab disunity. Both means had become discredited; not one inch of Palestine had been "liberated".

Out of the blue, the *intifada* broke away from this traditional attitude. It showed the world a new Palestinian face. The fearless young stone-throwers were neither bloodthirsty terrorists nor abject refugees, but—in the eyes of many previously unsympathetic to the Palestinians—patriots ready to die to end an unjust occupation. At the same time, they were expressing their refusal to go on waiting for the Arabs—or the PLO—to come to their rescue. The *intifada* was theirs. Its message was self-reliance, its goal self-determination.

It accordingly threw the PLO into some disarray. It was under great pressure to respond. But how? The eventual decision to proclaim an independent state of Palestine was the symbolic, and easy, part of its response. Arafat's statement, in December 1988 before the UN General Assembly, accepting Israel's existence and renouncing terrorism was much more painful. It strained the unity not just of the PLO as a whole but of Arafat's own group, *Fatah*, the movement's largest component. For one thing, Arafat's concessions followed some fairly public American pressure. For another, many doubted whether he would get anything substantial in return.

Arafat was caught between conflicting pressures, and his response was, characteristically, to take a major gamble. His aim was to try to assert the PLO's claim to full representation at an international peace conference and, beyond that, its claim to full statehood. But, despite the impact of the *intifada*, these claims were not universally acknowledged. The USA, to be sure, rewarded Arafat's new-found moderation by opening a "substantive" dialogue with the PLO. But it did so without endorsing the PLO's claim to be the sole legitimate representative of the Palestinian people, or its claim to an independent state. By mid-1989, there had been three formal rounds of the dialogue without any dramatic progress. The very fact that such a dialogue was taking place had shocked and alarmed Israel. But the Shamir government, after some initial confusion, responded shrewdly by proposing elections in Gaza and the West Bank designed to lead to a limited period of Palestinian self-rule—and to eventual negotiations on the final status of the territories. The proposal was quickly endorsed by President Bush in Washington, who sought a number of clarifications from Israel. Whether the plan was meant to be a genuine prelude to peace or, as its critics alleged, a ploy to take the heat off Israel, its effect was to divide Palestinians and to provide an uncomfortable test of Arafat's new moderation.

ISRAELI FEARS

Unlike most states, Israel is governed by the politics of fear. Its overiding imperative is survival. Objectively, its survival seems more than adequately assured by its own military strength—tested in five wars in as many decades—and that of its main ally, the USA. Nevertheless, subjectively, Israelis (and their friends abroad) fear not only the Arab armies or Arab terrorism but a host of other spectres—the rise of militant Islam, a resurgence of anti-Semitism, an eventual erosion of American support and, since the beginning of the *intifada*, the risk that the occupied territories could become completely ungovernable.

Because Israel is a contentious society which often engages in fierce and open debate, the unifying effect of these fears is sometimes underestimated. Thus it has become a cliché to observe that Israel is split into two opposing camps—"hawks" and "doves"—represented by the right-wing *Likud* Party (led by Itzhak Shamir) and the left-of-centre Labour Party (led by Shimon Peres). But the division, though real, is not as total as it sometimes seems. There are some issues which are seen as national rather than party-political. And it is essentially for this reason that the country has been governed since 1984 by *Likud*-Labour coalitions, under the label of "governments of national unity".

In the indecisive election of 1984, the dominant issue was the economy. Inflation had soared beyond 400 per cent a year, and it was felt that painful medicine could be administered more effectively by the two parties in tandem than by either one of them alone. The result was that short-term measures to tackle inflation were taken (with initial success) while, by mutual agreement, real structural reform of the economy was shelved. As the 1988 election drew nearer, members of both camps swore they would never get back into bed together, so frustrating had they found the experience of sharing power. But when that election too proved indecisive, lo and behold, another government of national unity was cobbled together—the main difference being that, this time, *Likud* was the dominant partner.

What, then, was the appeal of this two-headed monster which politicians and voters alike declared they were heartily sick of? The only satisfactory explanation seems to be that, in a country that was so badly polarized, a coalition government of this kind had proved a necessary instrument of indecision. On certain key questions—notably how to cure a sick economy and how to break the deadlock in the peace process—decisions were simply too painful and divisive. The only possible agreement was to put them off. Coalition government led, of course, to periodic rows and splits and difficulties. And the device often exasperated those countries—including the United States—which constantly urged Israel to take the tough decisions. But, unsatisfactory as coalition government clearly was, the alternatives were, in Israeli eyes, worse.

On the question of peace, while it is true to say that roughly half of all Israelis are ready to trade a large part of the occupied territories for peace, and that the other half wants to keep them as part of a "Greater Israel", that is not the whole story. On other important—and closely related—issues, there is a large degree of national (or at least bi-partisan) consensus. Two main features of that consensus are a basic determination to maintain a minimum of law and order in Gaza and the West Bank (i.e. to use military means to counter the *intifada*), and a basic distrust of the PLO's intentions (including a reluctance to accept the idea of a Palestinian state, whatever its territorial dimensions).

It is against this background that the impact of the *intifada* can be evaluated. It has certainly caused Israel a number of serious problems. Israel's repression of the uprising has earned it widespread international condemnation and has badly damaged its image. It has made it much harder for Israel to justify a policy of indefinite military occupation of the territories—whose Palestinian inhabitants are clearly united in opposing Israeli rule.

But the most germane question is surely this: has the *intifada* made Israelis readier to relinquish the territories? The uprising and its consequences—especially the withdrawal of Jordan as a potential negotiating partner, and the concomitant strengthening of the PLO—have sharpened Israel's dilemma. As a result, it seems to have made the "hawks" more "hawkish" and the "doves" more "dovish".

The point was underlined by the outcome of the 1988 election. Commentators described it as a referendum on whether Israel should hold on to the territories. But, if so, the electorate's response was: "We can't decide". And this inability to take the one central decision—a decision bound up with Israel's identity and indeed, in the opinion of many Israelis, Israel's very survival—was accurately reflected in the coalition government which eventually emerged from the election. To be sure, that coalition may not continue indefinitely, and if it collapses *Likud* seems more likely than Labour to emerge with a majority government (if, that is, any one party can secure a majority). But in the meantime, in a state still strongly motivated by fear, indecision has become institutionalized.

INTERNATIONAL INEPTITUDE

If two peoples can neither co-exist on the same piece of land nor divide it between them, surely the outside world needs to put forward solutions of its own. It seems only a slight exaggeration, however, to suggest that the long and bloody deadlock in the Middle East is the product not only of Arab weakness and Israeli fear but of international ineptitude, perhaps even international humbug.

Countries outside as well as inside the Middle East use the rhetoric of peace to cloak their own interests—and those interests are not, of course, identical.

For more than 20 years, the essential principle underlying the search for peace—and enshrined by the world community in UN Resolution 242 of 1967—has been that Israel should be guaranteed peace and security in return for relinquishing the territories it captured in the Six Day War of that year. Much has been made of the central ambiguity in Resolution 242. Does it mean all, or only some, of the captured territories? But it would be hard to claim that this ambiguity explains the failure to turn a cardinal principle—the exchange of land for peace—into a reality.

Resolution 242 does not exist in isolation. It is buttressed by other UN resolutions and by other key pronouncements—such as the European Community's Venice declaration of 1980, as well as statements made by the two superpowers and other permanent members of the UN Security Council. What emerges is an apparent consensus of long standing. There should be an international peace conference held under UN auspices, attended by the permanent members of the Security Council (the two superpowers and Britain, France and China) and by Israel, its Arab neighbours and the PLO (either separately or as part of a joint Arab delegation). The conference should—so the theory goes—lead to a negotiated Israeli withdrawal from all (or large parts) of the West Bank and Gaza Strip, and to agreement about the sovereignty of the Golan Heights and Jerusalem. In the relinquished territories, a Palestinian state (possibly federated or confederated with Jordan) should be established, and this state should live in peace with Israel—with mutual guarantees of security and some form of international supervision of their common border.

That, at least, has been the theory for more than two decades. This, apparently, is the type of formula—subject, of course, to modification in the course of negotiations—which the world community favours. It is a formula based on a *multilateral* approach to peace. Yet the peacemaking of the 1970s and '80s—notably the Camp David agreements of 1978—has done little more than pay lip-service to the multilateral ideal. President Jimmy Carter's achievement at Camp David was to achieve peace between Israel and Egypt. The hope was that this would provide the framework for a succession of further peace treaties. But this never happened. The peace process never got beyond the *bilateral* stage.

Three years after the Israeli–Egyptian peace treaty was signed in 1979, and following Israel's invasion of Lebanon and the trauma of the siege of Beirut in the summer of 1982, President Reagan announced a peace plan that was in several respects different from Carter's. The plan rejected indefinite Israeli control of the occupied territories, and it also rejected the creation of an independent Palestinian state. It called instead for an "association" between the West Bank and the kingdom of Jordan. Following the eruption of the *intifada*, Jordan's King Hussein relinquished his claim to the West Bank. This inevitably raised a question mark over Jordan's future role in the peace process. But Reagan's successor, George Bush, remained opposed to a Palestinian state and broadly committed to the Reagan plan. In welcoming Israeli Prime Minister Itzhak Shamir's proposal, put forward in early 1989, for local elections in the West Bank and Gaza, the American administration reiterated its reluctance to accept the idea of Palestinian self-determination—seeing this term as being synonymous with statehood. The preference in Washington seemed to be to encourage a step-by-step approach to negotiations, without prejudicing the final outcome, especially with regard to the sensitive question of sovereignty.

Other powers—notably the Soviet Union, Japan and the European Community—have not (in theory at least) shared this inhibition about Palestinian self-determination. But, in practice, they have all been influenced by what they know Israel and the United States will or will not accept. For Japan and the Europeans, two somewhat conflicting interests are at stake. The main one is economic. They are heavily dependent on Middle East (meaning Arab and Iranian) oil, and the region is also an important market for their exports (including arms). But their other interest is that they cannot afford to be too sharply at odds with the United States, whose political and strategic interests in the region are much bigger than their own. Thus these two sets of interest have tended, in practice, to neutralize one another. The commitment to Palestinian self-determination, in other words, remains largely theoretical.

Soviet interests are different only in so far as the Soviet Union is geographically closer to the region. It has several Moslem neighbours, as well as a large Moslem minority of its own, and therefore tends to see the Middle East as a volatile part of its backyard. Yet, like the Japanese and the Europeans, it too tends to view the region to a large extent in the context of its relations with Washington. Since the coming to power of Mikhail Gorbachev in 1985, this relationship has become less confrontational. Gorbachev insists he no longer sees the world in "zero-sum" terms (in other words, as a game in which one player's gain is always, and by definition, at his adversary's expense). This approach has led to the Soviet withdrawal from Afghanistan, and has encouraged efforts to solve "regional conflicts" (for example, in southern Africa) through joint superpower action—often in the context of diplomacy at the UN Security Council. In 1987, for example, both superpowers pushed for a Security Council resolution on a Gulf war ceasefire—and their concerted action undoubtedly contributed to the pressure which led to such a ceasefire the following year.

How realistic is it to expect similar progress in the Arab–Israeli conflict? Gorbachev has shown that he can often break the deadlock by making dramatic concessions, whether in arms-reduction talks or by his decision (essentially a political rather than military one) to pull his troops out of Afghanistan. In the Middle East, he has perhaps less scope for the dramatic gesture. One important card he can play is to renew the diplomatic relations with Israel which Moscow broke off at the time of the 1967 war in the Middle East. But it's a card he can only play once. So far, his gradual warming of relations with Israel has aroused remarkably little Arab opposition. While his main Arab ally, Syria, is clearly unhappy about it, most of the Arabs—including Arafat's PLO—realize that pressure by *both* superpowers will be necessary if Israel is ever to come to the peace table.

By mid-1989 it was clear that a potential deal was in the making. Gorbachev would renew diplomatic relations with Israel, and allow more Soviet Jews to emigrate, provided that Israel agreed to the kind of international conference Moscow was proposing.

No Israeli government could afford to ignore such inducements. Yet, what could Gorbachev do if Israel continued to resist an international conference—and if Washington (lukewarm about such a proposal) continued to explore bilateral, rather than multilateral, approaches to peace? Such a scenario indeed looked quite likely. The Bush administration made it clear, in June 1989, that it regarded the Soviet response to the idea of Palestinian local elections as a test of the new Gorbachev approach to solving regional conflicts. So this posed the question: if he remained in power (a much-debated question), how far would Gorbachev be prepared to go? Moscow's initial reaction was to reject the idea of elections, and then to describe the proposal as "interesting". The Soviet—and indeed the Arab—response seemed to depend on the *context* in which elections were to be held. In other words, how strong was the linkage between the elections and the all-important negotiations to achieve a settlement?

A FINAL ASSESSMENT

What, then, has been the overall effect of the Palestinian uprising? Paradoxically, it may well have changed everything and nothing. It has changed perceptions, both inside and outside the Middle East. It has changed the nature of the daily encounters between Israelis and Palestinians. It has brought home to many that the price of the *status quo* is dangerously high.

But has it, ultimately, provided a way out of the tunnel? The changes that have taken place between 1987 and 1989 have been remarkable. Few observers could have predicted them. But, by themselves, they do not necessarily constitute a breakthrough towards peace. Such a breakthrough would require:

i   a significant change of heart on the part of the majority of Israelis, enabling them to take a gamble for peace;

ii   a readiness by the United States to make its preferences clear not only to Israel but to the powerful pro-Israel lobby in America;

iii a greater degree of unanimity among Palestinians—not only between traditional "moderates" and "radicals", but between those inside and those outside the occupied territories;

iv   a greater degree of Arab unanimity—in particular, including Syria, which retains to some extent the ability to sabotage a peace treaty not to its liking;

v   continuing, or greater, superpower co-operation to solve this—and other—regional conflicts; and

vi   the absence (or at least the mitigation) of conflict elsewhere in the
     region—whether in the Gulf, Lebanon or elsewhere.

There are some observers who find grounds for optimism in the new
perceptions created by the *intifada*, and the possibilities for international
peace created by a period of superpower détente.

In the Middle East, however, perhaps more than in other regional
conflicts, there are many issues, many actors, many complications, many
things that can go wrong. In theory, the conditions set out above (and the
list is far from exhaustive) may yet be fulfilled. In practice, it seems a tall
order.

Israeli settlers stepping out (*Tordai*)

Schoolgirls confronting Border Police, Jerusalem (*Tordai*)

REPORTAGE

JERUSALEM DIVIDED

Paul Cossali

"There's no *intifada* in Jerusalem," is a comment one sometimes hears from Palestinians. It's usually said as an expression of disappointment or frustration that the intended capital of a future Palestinian state can feel so relaxed compared to other parts of the occupied territories. As sentiment it's understandable, but as a prelude to analysis it ignores the transformation undergone by the Arab half of Jerusalem since the uprising began. For more than a year and a half the city's rhythms have been set by the directives of the uprising's underground leadership. Midday in east Jerusalem is sounded by the clanging of a thousand metal shutters as the entire city shuts up shop in observance of the afternoon's commercial strike. Simultaneously schoolkids stream out and onto the streets in what has become an automatic act of solidarity with the merchants and café owners. Later on in the day the same children don masks and arm themselves with rocks and bottles to harry the Israeli buses, whose night-time routes take them through the Arab quarters.

What is undeniably true, however, is that the *intifada* in Jerusalem lacks the same intensity as elsewhere. One morning, I watched as a group of girls started a demonstration on their way to school. They blocked the street with overturned rubbish carts and began half-hearted chanting. Most of their classmates filed past with their heads down. After a couple of minutes a police van approached and drove, cautiously at first, towards the demonstrators. Once the point was reached when it was clear to both parties that stones were not going to be thrown, the van disgorged a couple of fat policemen who barked an order for the girls to go home. Sheepishly they complied. A Palestinian friend fresh from Nablus who had seen the incident unfold could hardly conceal his disgust.

In a sense this milder form of militancy is only to be expected. Having been annexed, albeit illegally, to the Jewish State, Jerusalem has been cushioned from the worst excesses of military rule which did so much to create the uprising in the West Bank and Gaza. Combine this with the city's relative affluence, transient population and less cohesive community structures and you have an environment which the underground committees, the driving motor of the *intifada*, find difficult to penetrate.

There are numerous tell-tale signs which point to the weakness of the committee structure in Jerusalem. Graffiti are patchy, rents have not been lowered in line with the directives of the United Leadership and the shops are still stocked with the Israeli goods which were burned in Nablus months before. Without strong committees it's been difficult to organize the daily round of street clashes which are the most potent reminder to Palestinians, Israelis and the outside world alike, that the *intifada* is alive and kicking. Jerusalem is probably unique in the occupied territories as the only place where general strikes are accompanied by a drop in tension. Twenty kilometres up the road in Ramallah, strike days draw a faithful band of journalists to witness a guaranteed game of cat and mouse played out between the army and members of the "popular strike forces". On the same day in Jerusalem, one colleague complained, "you could die of boredom".

The problem facing *intifada* activists are magnified by the fact that for the Israelis themselves, too much is at stake in Jerusalem to let the situation get out of hand. If their claim to sovereignty over the Palestinian half of the city is to have any credibility in the international arena, then it's essential that there is a quiet of sorts on the eastern front. There are economic as well as political imperatives. If Gaza or Nablus are burning, it affects the all-important tourist revenues, but the damage is limited because neither place has ever figured on any visitor's itinerary. But take a glance at any Israeli tourist brochure and it becomes clear that Jerusalem, more than Tel Aviv or Eilat, is the country's principal selling point. And that's the east of the city, not the Israeli west. No tourist official with hand on heart could claim that the indifferent architecture and suburban atmosphere of west Jerusalem has ever compared in the tourist mind with the Biblical sites and assorted exotica of the "Old City" in the east.

So, ever since December 1987 when the first shock waves of the *intifada* reached the city and produced the most committed rioting in 20 years of occupation, Israel's Defence Ministry has taken care and expense to ensure that such an outburst would never be repeated. Massive numbers of security personnel have been drafted into the area; border guards stand sentinel over the ramparts of the Old City like toy soldiers atop a fort, police vans patrol with monotonous regularity day and night, and the plainclothes police in their jeans and T-shirt uniform with strategic bulges lurk like pimps in the alleyways. If this isn't sufficient to deter protest, then the practice is to quell street demonstrations by force of numbers rather than by a liberal use of live ammunition as happens elsewhere. Deaths are bad for business, and Jerusalem demonstrators are probably the only Palestinians who ever see their adversaries carrying riot shields.

Yet for all their successes in keeping the violence in Jerusalem at a manageable level, Israel's security forces have been impotent to bridge the psychological gulf that the *intifada* has opened between the two halves of the city. Even on the best of pre-*intifada* days, contact between the Palestinian and Israeli citizens of the city was largely restricted to commercial transactions, but now the sabbath shoppers and the hunters after cheap vegetables stay on their own side of the Green Line. The only Israelis not in uniform who venture into Palestinian areas of the east are the nationalist militants who have established mini-colonies in the Old City. And when they go out shopping they always take their Uzis with them.

LESSONS OF THE HOLOCAUST

Elfi Pallis

Tel Aviv does not know any spring, just a long summer that starts around March and abruptly ends in November with floods of cold rain, but as I stepped from my hotel into another sweltering May day the sudden wail of sirens made me shiver. Having lived away from Israel for so long, it took me a moment to recall that the sounds coming from several directions marked the beginning of Holocaust Day.

For the next three minutes, the bustling city stood still. Cars and passers-by stopped in their tracks. Nobody talked. Then the sounds petered out again, everyone hurried on and the horrors that ended over forty years ago receded into the distance for most people. After all, only 10 per cent of today's Israelis lived through them, and the country's oriental Jewish majority is not even tied to them through the loss of relations.

Nevertheless, opinions I was to subsequently hear convinced me that the holocaust still casts a heavy shadow over Israeli society. Keeping the painful memories alive has always been official policy for ideological reasons reiterated not long ago by Defence Minister Itzhak Rabin. When visiting the site of Dachau concentration camp as guest of the German government, he declared that Israel itself was the lesson of the holocaust. To remember was to understand the need for the country's existence.

Some prominent Israeli intellectuals, however, nowadays argue that if there is indeed any holocaust lesson to be learnt, it must deal with the kind of state Israel should be after those terrible events. Playwright Yeshua Sobol likes to emphasize that this is not an abstract question, given that Israel now rules over a large ethnic minority, and its harsh repression of the *intifada* has fuelled the debate.

Sobol warns that by dispossessing Palestinians, and "holding their young men in prison camps or closing off their townships so that they become ghettoes", Israelis are subconsciously accepting some values of their former tormentors. In the same vein, writer Levi Itzhak Yerushalmi has claimed that Israel's bombing of civilians in Lebanon implied that "it is permissible to spill blood, kill and destroy without restraint and beyond reason, as long as one does not do it to one's own people or race".

Like Sobol, Yerushalmi attributes much of this thinking to holocaust suffering. Writer Boaz Evron has gone further in blaming not just the holocaust itself, but the use Israeli public figures make of it. The country's schools and politicians, he says, not so much preserve the memory of the holocaust as distort it. Instead of describing what happened between 1933 and 1945 as the murder of six million European Jews, as well as of millions of Slavs and Gypsies, by a German fascist regime in specific historic circumstances, they talk of the "Shoah" (the Hebrew term for holocaust), as the symbol of Jewish destiny.

Such an approach actually endangers Israel, warns Evron. By taking genocide as the norm, Israelis become incapable of sensible political conduct. They see most non-Jews as implacable racists who can only be kept at bay through military strength. Worst of all, the wars between Israel and the Arab states are perceived as "an expression of the Jewish fate" rather than a territorial conflict, and the bitter but rational hostility of the displaced Palestinians is seen as gentile anti-Semitism. "For many Israelis", says Evron, "there is no difference between a Palestinian peasant refugee and a member of the SS".

A look through the Israeli press reveals that such an approach is even taken by politicians who knew Europe during Nazism. Polish-born former Premier Menahem Begin refers to the PLO as the "Nazi Murderers' Organization", and has described Israel's 1982 invasion of Beirut as "the march on Berlin". His successor Itzhak Shamir has continued to compare Arafat to Hitler even after the PLO recognized Israel in 1988. Far from docile but undoubtedly oppressed, the Palestinians remain timeless manifestations of evil to most Israelis.

Some Israelis believe that more information about the "real" holocaust will help to put things into perspective, but this is disputed by novelist Dan Ben Amotz, who feels that too much detail is counter-productive. "By burying us in a welter of gory details", argues the writer, whose parents were shot in the leafy park of his Polish home town, "the powers-that-be are obscuring, perhaps deliberately, the awful fact that it was ordinary people like us who signed expulsion orders, sealed confiscated houses, put people on trucks, expropriated their property, ticked race or nationality on their papers, drove the trains eastwards or stood aloof and generally did what was expected of them".

What else they could have done was suggested to me later on that remembrance day while having tea with Professor Israel Shahak, scientist and chairman of Israel's Human and Civil Rights League, who was liberated at the age of 12 from Bergen Belsen. Surrounded by files documenting the arrest, torture and killing of Palestinians, he had no doubt about where his sympathies should lie. Recalling a childhood spent under occupation, he stressed that he, like other Jewish children, was hidden by Poles for a time, despite the risks this entailed. On the values behind such acts he quoted the Polish labourer who had rebuked a workmate for saying that it was a good thing the Germans were ridding Poland of Jews with the words: "Fear God! Are they not also human beings?"

REFERENCE SECTION

POPULATION

According to official Israeli estimates, the total population of Israel at the end of 1987 was 4,406,500 (including East Jerusalem, the Golan Heights and Israeli settlers in the occupied territories): the Palestinian population of the occupied territories was 1,125,000.

The principal population centres are as follows (figures from the 1983 census):

Jerusalem	428,668
Tel-Aviv–Jaffa	327,625
Haifa	235,775
Holon	132,460

ECONOMIC ACTIVITY

INDUSTRY AND AGRICULTURE

Israel has a highly developed agricultural sector, with its scientists at the forefront of research in desert agriculture. Among its principal crops are citrus fruits, vegetables and wheat. Apart from limited phosphate and potash mining, there is no extractive industry.

Leading industrial products include diamond cutting, liquified petroleum gases, ammonia, polythene, vegetable oils, paper and board.

Large numbers of Palestinians from the territories commute to work within Israel, although this has declined as a result of the *intifada*. Independent Palestinian economic activity is to some extent restricted by legal and informal restraints. Small-scale industries on the West Bank include agricultural processing, canning and packaging operations. Olives, fruit and vegetables are among the principal agricultural products, as well as sheep and goats.

EXTERNAL TRADE

Israel's leading exports are processed diamonds, machinery and parts, metals, fruit and vegetables (notably citrus fruits). Imports include rough diamonds, machinery, chemicals and petroleum.

Its main trading partners are the USA, Britain, West Germany, Belgium and Luxembourg.

POLITICAL STRUCTURE: ISRAEL

CONSTITUTION

The State of Israel is a multi-party democracy, with a President elected by Parliament for a five-year term, a government under a Prime Minister and a unicameral 120-member Parliament (*Knesset*), elected for a four-year term by universal suffrage of all citizens of 18 years and above. The Cabinet is responsible to the *Knesset*. The right to vote does not extend to Palestinian residents of the occupied territories. Candidates for the *Knesset* are elected by proportional representation from party lists, with the whole country forming a single constituency and with a list requiring at least 1 per cent of the votes cast to secure representation.

The present coalition government, as established in December 1988, is composed as follows:

Itzhak Shamir (*Likud*)*	Prime Minister; Minister Labour
Shimon Peres (Align.)*	Vice Prime Minister; Minister of Finance
David Levi (*Likud*)*	Second Vice Prime Minister; Minister of Housing and Construction
Itzhak Navon (Align.)*	Deputy Prime Minister; Minister of Education and Culture
Moshe Arens (*Likud*)*	Foreign Affairs
Itzhak Rabin (Align.)*	Defence
Moshe Katsav (*Likud*)	Transport
Chaim Bar-Lev (Align.)*	Police
Ariel Sharon (*Likud*)*	Trade and Industry
Moshe Shahal (Align.)	Energy and Infrastructure
Dan Meridor (*Likud*)	Justice
Avraham Katz-Oz (Align.)	Agriculture
Gideon Patt (*Likud*)	Tourism
Yaacov Tsur (Align.)	Health
Zevulun Hammer (NRP)	Religious Affairs
Itzhak Moda'i (*Likud*)*	Economy and Planning
Gad Yaakobi (Align.)	Communications
Arie Der'i (*Shas*)	Interior
Itzhak Peretz (*Shas*)	Integration of Immigrants
Ezer Weizmann (Align.)*	Science and Technology
Ronni Milo (*Likud*)	Environmental Quality

Moshe Nissim (*Likud*)*	Without Portfolio
Ehud Olmert (*Likud*)	Without Portfolio
Mordechai Gur (Align.)	Without Portfolio
Rafi Edri (Align.)	Without Portfolio

*Members of the inner Cabinet

Political Parties

The party political scene in Israel is somewhat ephemeral, with new parties frequently being formed and inter-party alliances shifting. The majority of minor parties lend their support to one or other of the main groupings. In the November 1988 election, 15 parties won representation in the *Knesset*, as follows:

Likud (40 seats). Founded in 1973 on the basis of the right-wing *Herut*, which was itself set up by Menahem Begin in 1948, the *Likud* Front stands for a free enterprise economy in a unified *"Eretz Israel"*, including the West Bank and Gaza. *Leader*: Itzhak Shamir.

Labour (39 seats). Set up in 1968, as a result of the merger of *Mapai* and smaller factions, Labour is a "democratic socialist" party favouring centralized control of the economy. It has organic links with the *Histadrut*, the trade union federation. Labour believes in territorial compromise as a means of achieving peace with Arab states and the Palestinians. *Leader*: Shimon Peres.

Shas International Organization of Torah-Observant Sephardic Jews (6 seats). The ultra-Orthodox *Shas* was founded in 1984 as a breakaway from *Agudat Israel* (see below). It is "guided and directed" by the Council of Torah Scholars. *Leader*: Itzhak Peretz.

Ratz Civil Rights and Peace Movement (5 seats). Founded in 1973, *Ratz* supports women's rights and freedom for the individual from the religious establishment. It is strongly opposed to *Likud* policies toward the Palestinians. *Leader*: Shulamit Aloni.

National Religious Party (5 seats). The NRP was founded in 1956 as a religious Zionist party which seeks "the renewal of the life of the Jewish people in the (Biblical) Land of Israel according to the Torah". It supports the expansion of settlement activity. *Leader*: Rabbi Itzhak Levi.

Agudat Israel Union of Israel (5 seats). The Party stands for strict observance of Jewish religious law, to be backed by state legislation. Founded in 1912, it has recently, in common with other religious parties, tended to align itself with the *Likud*. All decisions are subject to approval by a Council of Sages (rabbis). *Leader*: Pinhas Menachem Alter.

Democratic Front for Peace and Equality *Hadash* (4 seats). The DFPE was set up in 1977 as an alliance of the New Communist (*Rakah*) and (Sephardic Jewish) Black Panthers. It enjoys wide support among Israeli Arabs, and favours the formation of a Palestinian state in the West Bank and Gaza. *Leaders*: Meir Vilner, Tawfik Toubi (*Rakah*); Charlie Biton (Black Panthers).

Tehiya Zionist Revival Movement (3 seats). The far-right *Tehiya* wants increased settlement activity and the declaration of Israeli sovereignty over the occupied territories.

Mapam United Workers Party (3 seats). Founded in 1948, the leftist *Mapam* was linked to Labour as part of the Alignment from 1969 to 1984, when it broke away over the coalition agreement. It seeks a peace settlement on the basis of the "Jordanian option".

Centre Party (2 seats). Launched in February 1988 in opposition to the coalition, it includes Labour and *Likud* dissidents based around the old *Shinui* ("Change") Party, among them Moshe Amirav, expelled from *Likud* for talking to PLO supporters.

Moledet Homeland (2 seats). Led by Gen. Rechavam Ze'evi, "Homeland" demands the expulsion of Palestinians from the West Bank and Gaza.

Tzomet Renewed Zionism Party (2 seats). Set up by former Chief of Staff Gen. Rafael Eitan in 1983, the far-right *Tzomet* campaigns for Israeli sovereignty over all of *Eretz Israel*.

Degal Hatora Guardians of the Torah (2 seats). A Western Jewish breakaway from *Agudat Israel* (see above), established in 1988.

Progressive List for Peace (1 seat). Founded jointly by a Palestinian (Mohammed Miari) and a Jewish Israeli (Mattiyahu Peled) in 1983, the PLP advocates recognition of the PLO and the establishment of a Palestinian state in the West Bank and Gaza.

Arab Democratic Party (1 seat). Set up in 1988 by ex-Labour member Abdel Wahab Darwish, the ADP supports recognition of the PLO and Israeli withdrawal from all occupied territories.

POLITICAL STRUCTURE:
PALESTINE LIBERATION ORGANIZATION

The PLO is, in effect, the sole Palestinian political organization, operating as an "umbrella" network grouping together guerrilla groups and other political, social and cultural bodies. It is a banned organization within Israel and the occupied territories.

The PLO was set up in 1964 after an Arab League initiative sponsored by President Nasser. The first session of what later became known as the Palestine National Council—the PLO's "parliament-in-exile"—was held in east (Jordanian) Jerusalem in May–June 1964. It took the decision to form the PLO as "the only legitimate spokesman for all matters concerning the Palestinian people". It adopted the "National Charter" (recently described as "obsolete" by Arafat, see above) calling for the liberation of all Palestine by "armed struggle".

In general terms, the PNC, composed of guerrilla faction members and independent figures, decides on broad strategic policy, with more tactical matters being decided by the PLO Executive Committee. There is also a PLO Central Council, which acts as an advisory body.

PRINCIPAL PLO FACTIONS:

Al-Fatah: Tahir al-Hatani al Falastani—Movement for the National Liberation of Palestine. "*Al-Fatah*" can be translated as "victory". Founded in the late 1950s. By far the largest of the Palestinian guerrilla groups, led by PLO Chairman Yasser Arafat, *Fatah* is a relatively moderate, non-ideological nationalist grouping. Division in the wake of the Lebanese war resulted in the formation in 1983 of a Syrian-backed "*Fatah Revolutionary Council*", (known as the "*Fatah rebels*") led by Saed (Abu) Musa, which opposes Arafat's leadership.

Popular Front for the Liberation of Palestine. Notionally of Marxist-Leninist orientation. Founded by Georges Habash, a Christian Arab, in

1967, the PFLP was responsible for much of the Palestinian "terrorist" activities of the late 1960s and early 1970s. In recent years, Habash has been highly critical of Arafat's leadership, although he accepted the decisions of the 19th PNC.

Democratic Front for the Liberation of Palestine. Split from the PFLP in 1969. Led by Naif Hawatmeh (also a Christian), the DFLP's radical Marxist bias has softened in recent years with Hawatmeh working to foster PLO unity. The group has developed contacts with left-wing Israelis, and favours the establishment of a single democratic state of Palestine for both Jews and Arabs.

Popular Front for the Liberation of Palestine–General Command. Another breakaway from the PFLP (in 1968) the PFLP–GC was also responsible for a number of terrorist-style attacks in the early 1970s. It demands the destruction of Israel and as such is implacably opposed to Arafat's diplomatic approach. Led by Ahmed Jabril, a former Syrian Army officer, the PFLP–GC enjoys substantial Syrian support.

"Abu Nidal Group". Revolutionary Council of *Fatah*. Known by the code name of its leader and founder, Sabri Khalil al-Banna, the Abu Nidal Group was set up in Iraq in 1973. It later came under Syrian influence, and became notorious during the early 1980s for its attacks on PLO moderates. It was also widely blamed for the 1982 assassination of Israel's Ambassador to London (which sparked the Lebanese invasion) and the 1985 Rome and Vienna airport attacks. In the late 1980s, however, the Group has reportedly adopted a more moderate approach in line with the PLO leadership.

Al-Saiqa *The Storm.* Founded by the Syrian government in 1968 as a counterweight to *Al-Fatah*. After a period of "moderation" in the 1970s, *Saiqa* is now one of the three remaining "rejectionist" groups (together with the PFLP–GC and "*Fatah* rebels"), firmly opposed to current PLO policy.

Palestine Liberation Front. The PLF was set up by Talat Yacoub in 1977 as a breakaway from the PFLP–GC. After it came out against the mainstream PLO leadership in the early 1980s, a rival pro-Arafat PLF was established under Mahmoud Abul Abbas. It was this wing which staged the *Achille Lauro* hijack—widely condemned by the rest of the

PLO. The PLF is now broadly reunified and accepts mainstream PLO policy.

Palestine Popular Struggle Front.   An Iraqi-backed group set up in 1968. Part of the "rejection front" during the late 1970s and early 1980s, the PPSF had effectively resumed its place in the PLO mainstream by 1988, under the leadership of Samir Ghosheh.

Political Organization within "Palestine"

In the wake of the *intifada*, the effective political leadership of the uprising in the occupied territories is exercised by underground bodies, notably the United National Leadership network, predominantly on the West Bank, and the Islamic *Hamas* and Jihad, which are particularly strong in the Gaza Strip. At grassroots level, their decisions are enforced by semi-clandestine "popular committees". These are most influential in the refugee camps.

All these organizations express loyalty to the PLO.

INDEX